BECOMING the BEST

A Journey *of* Passion, Purpose, *and* Perseverance

RICHARD M. SCHULZE

FOUNDER AND CHAIRMAN, BEST BUY CO., INC.

This edition of
Becoming the Best: A Journey of Passion, Purpose, and Perseverance
is privately published by Richard M. Schulze.

Second reprint, May 2017

This book was created in collaboration with the author by Idea Platforms, Inc.

Idea Platforms

One Main Street, Suite 1370
Cambridge, MA 02142
www.ideaplatforms.com

Produced by
Sideshow Media, LLC
www.sideshowbooks.com

Printed and bound in the United States of America

CONTENTS

To Best Buy employees—
former, current, and future.
Wishing all to be the best they can be.

FOREWORD

MANY FRIENDS AND ASSOCIATES HAVE ASKED ME WHY I took so long to write the history and lessons learned over my forty-six-year journey with the company. My response has always been, "I'll get to it. Maybe when I'm seventy." I guess my continued involvement as chairman and the ongoing challenges Best Buy faces have kept me focused on the present and the future rather than on the past.

As the years went by, however, I began to realize that our company has become so large and spread out around the world that only a small number of employees really know the full story of the company. I decided it was important to describe how we built Best Buy into the company it is today, so all our people could understand what it took to create the best-in-class company we have become.

Today, we are one of the Fortune 50, a leader in our industry. We operate out of a magnificent world headquarters in Minnesota, and we employ some 180,000 people worldwide. As you'll see, however, we were quite a different company when this journey began in 1966.

Ours is a story of continuous improvement. In order to grow and improve, our leaders have never been afraid to get their hands dirty, to help others when called upon, and to pitch in to manage any important undertaking. We have been blessed with two wonderfully talented CEOs who followed me, and they have led us through some very complex and interesting times. Brad Anderson took the reins in 2002 and led the customer centricity initiative, transforming us from a product-centric company to a customer-centric enterprise. Brian Dunn, who assumed the role of CEO in 2009, has forged the path to a "connected world"—providing products and services that enable customers to engage with real-time information, communication, and entertainment wherever they are, at any time of the day or night.

As important as our leaders have been to our success, this is equally a story of ordinary people working together and accomplishing extraordinary things, especially when challenged. Best Buy is about empowering employees to become all they can be—by engaging, growing, and sharing their learnings with one another.

Throughout our journey, I have lived by a simple mantra: Best Buy is a community of four constituencies, all of them important to our success:

Customers. We work continually to serve them better.

Employees. We empower them. We enable them to develop into the best they can be. We give them the opportunity to advance their careers.

Suppliers. It is their skills in the design of technology and innovation that drive our business. The partnerships we make with them bring great benefit to the Best Buy community.

Shareholders. They've helped us expand, grow, and develop best-in-class infrastructure.

As you read this book, you'll understand the importance of building winning relationships for all four constituencies, without which successful outcomes will not be sustainable.

Finally, I must touch upon the personal aspect of the Best Buy story. My late wife, Sandy, and our four children—Susan, Debra,

Nancy, and Rick—helped me over the many hurdles I faced and never lost confidence in me or my dream for the future. After Sandy died of a rare cancer, God blessed me with a second wonderful spouse, Maureen. We have been married for nearly ten years now, and our family numbers ten wonderful children and twenty-four grandchildren. Each has a unique personality, and we are proud of every one of them. I am truly blessed to have had their love and support. I am also blessed to have been associated with all the employees of Best Buy, one of the best—and biggest—families anyone could ever have.

If it all ended tomorrow, I know that through Best Buy, I have been able to make a tremendous and positive impact on the lives of many, many people, and for that I am truly grateful.

DESTINY

I WON'T CLAIM THAT EVERYTHING I KNOW ABOUT BUSINESS I learned as a paperboy, but it's not far from the truth.

So I'll begin this book by telling you a bit about my early life, because I learned some very important lessons then, and with a few additions and modifications, they have served me well throughout the years—both personally and as founder and leader of the company that is now Best Buy.

But don't worry—this is not a history exercise. Although I'll tell stories from my own life and talk about some of the key moments in our company's development, I'm really talking about Best Buy *today*—and tomorrow. The lessons I have learned still very much apply to our business right now. And if followed—well, these lessons will ensure that we continue to be one of the greatest companies on earth for a long time to come.

Of course, I knew none of that back in 1952. That's the year I started out, at age eleven, as a newspaper carrier. My family—my father, mother, twin sister, and two kid brothers—lived in a modest three-bedroom house at 2135 St. Clair Avenue in the Groveland Park section of St. Paul, Minnesota. At the height of my newspaper business, I was delivering the paper to 126 families in a ten-block area around our house every day, including Sunday—the *Pioneer Press* in the morning and the *St. Paul Dispatch* in the afternoon.

My father was of German descent, a very precise person and a strict disciplinarian. He was always focused on getting things done properly and on time. He also believed that the children in our family should contribute to the expenses of the household, and required that we pay 20 percent of our earnings into the family kitty. In my best years as a paperboy, I earned between $104 and $106 a month, which meant that at least $20 went to helping our family of six with food and rent and other monthly living expenses. I didn't complain. My sister, Judie, also kicked in 20 percent of the money she made from her babysitting jobs. That's just the way it was. (Even so, I've always suspected that my father went a little easier on my brothers, Jim and Bob, who were five and nine years younger than me. But I guess that's the way it goes for the older children.)

I took my newspaper business pretty seriously and always thought about the best way to get the job done. The houses on my route were on both sides of the street, which ran down a fairly steep hill. I figured out that the fastest and least tiring way to deliver the papers was to break the job into pieces. I'd start with the heaviest load I could carry, move to the top of the hill and work my way down, going from side to side, crossing and recrossing the street. When I ran out of papers, I'd reload my bag and climb back to where I had left off. By breaking down the job into smaller parts, varying the work by crossing the street—rather than going down one side and up the other—and by getting a little help from gravity, I found that my modest entrepreneurial business was quite profitable, even with that 20 percent "family tax."

As with any business, there were some special complications with mine. In the Twin Cities, winter was the toughest. The temperature could drop to thirty below zero, and the snow on the ground could often be measured not in inches, but in feet. Everybody had different shoveling habits, which meant I couldn't always follow my standard delivery routine, but would navigate from cleared patch to cleared patch. If a stretch of sidewalk hadn't been shoveled at all, I just had to plow my way through. That slowed me down. If there was a lot of snow everywhere, I'd pile the papers on my sled—especially on Sunday, when the weight of the paper was about five times that of the weekday edition. The sled helped, but it slowed me down, too.

In those first couple of years of tending to my paper route, I became a reasonably independent person and careful thinker. I looked hard at the job and kept asking myself questions: *Does what I'm doing feel right? If not, what's wrong with it? What could I do differently or better or faster?* I didn't have the business vocabulary then, but already I was looking for ways to increase efficiency and improve produc-tivity. And I did. By the time I moved on to other jobs, I had gotten the paper-carrying business pretty much down to a science.

My biggest and most memorable lesson came when I was fifteen. I was a sophomore in high school and decided it was time for my first date. The most logical occasion would be the spring prom. The only honorable (and macho) way to take a date to the prom was in a car, but I didn't have one. I didn't even have my license. So, that fall, thinking well ahead, I asked my father if he would let me borrow his car at prom time. His immediate answer was *no*.

"You're not old enough," he said. "Your mother and I will drive you. I'll let you know when it's time for you to drive a car." (In his defense, I should say that my father used the family car for his work as a manufacturer's rep in the electronics business. He couldn't risk me cracking it up.)

Dad's reaction, however, did not discourage me. In fact, it inspired me. If he wouldn't lend me his car, I'd find a way to get my own. No way was I going on my first date—to the prom, no less—with my father at the wheel and my mother in the front seat beside him! All I had to do was increase my income, just enough to afford a used vehicle. But how could I do that? I didn't control the price of the newspaper. That was fixed. I'd have to find another way.

I thought long and hard about what I could do. I made my collections once a month; looking ahead, I realized that December's collection week fell at Christmastime. My customers would sometimes tip me, and often they would up the amount during the holiday season. I decided that the best strategy for increasing my income was to improve my holiday delivery service in hopes of getting bigger tips.

My plan was simple. Usually, like every paper carrier both then and now, I would throw the newspaper from the sidewalk and it would land somewhere in the vicinity of the customer's porch or doorway. Customers might grumble about the placement, especially when it was snowing and they had to come out in their bare feet or dig out the paper from under the snow. I guessed they would really like it if I brought the paper right up the steps and tucked it inside the storm door. So, starting on Thanksgiving and continuing through the day before Christmas, I took the extra time and trouble to walk up the steps and carefully place the paper out of the weather, within easy reach, warm and dry and all set to read. This "enhanced service" added no more than fifteen minutes to the total time it took me to complete my route.

The strategy worked like a charm. My customers were ecstatic. I still remember counting out the tips I collected in the few days before Christmas—a grand total of $300. It was just enough to purchase a 1950 Pontiac straight-stick, six-cylinder, two-door sedan from Arrow Pontiac on University Avenue in St. Paul. I handled the entire transaction myself, without any help from my father. He did teach me to drive, though, which involved quite a bit of bumping and jumping before I mastered the art of shifting. I got my driver's license on my fifteenth birthday: January 2, 1956.

It was an exciting time for me. I had learned how to drive, earned my license, and bought a car all in one month. Now I had the distinction of being one of the few sophomores at St. Paul Central High School who owned a car. Because the Pontiac was a two-toned job, dark green on top and light green on the bottom, we called it the Green Hornet, in honor of the masked superhero character that is still going strong today.

No longer did I have to hitchhike to school or, if I couldn't catch a ride, trudge the three and a half miles each way. For the rest of my high school career, I operated on my own time and made my own schedule. It was a great feeling. I can still remember how special it was to load my friends into the car after school and drop them off at their houses on my way back home. An added bonus was that my younger brothers loved to wash the car. (Delegation is always a good practice.) And I proudly escorted my date to the prom that May 1956, just as I had planned.

I said that I had learned important lessons in those years, and I did, but I had no big ambition then—beyond taking my date to the prom. I had no idea that I would start a business when I got older, let alone that I would be involved in creating a Fortune 100 company known around the world. There was one thing I did know, however, and I knew it to the very bottom of my heart: I wanted to control my own destiny. I wasn't exactly sure how things would play out. I didn't even have a particular career plan or business in mind. All I knew was that I wanted to be in control of who I was, who I would be, and what I would do. I wanted to do things as I thought they should be done. If that included making mistakes, so be it. But my success, if it was to come, would be my own. I knew I would learn by trying new ways.

Well, success did come—for me and for all of us. As I write this book (and I wouldn't be writing a book at all if we *hadn't* been successful), Best Buy operates more than four thousand stores in fourteen countries around the world. We employ about 180,000 people, and in 2010 we took in nearly $50 billion in revenue. We are the number one company in our specialty business—consumer electronics, personal computers, major appliances, digital imaging, and entertainment software.

One of the challenges facing companies of our size is that they often forget their roots, lose sight of their values, and ignore the lessons that made them great. So my purpose in writing this book is to tell stories that remind us of our roots (they're pretty humble, really), to describe some of the most critical moments in our development that demonstrate the incredible importance of values, and to draw out key lessons that I believe we all can benefit from and that will help us overcome any and every challenge we face in the future, no matter what it is. I believe that these lessons will enable us to do the same thing I wanted to do as a kid: *control our destiny*. If we don't, you can be sure that someone else will.

I think of this book as part of my legacy to the company that we all care so much about. Thank you for reading it.

CHAPTER ONE

THE EARLY DAYS

*Stuff Happens,
But Perseverance Pays*

I WOULD LIKE TO BE ABLE TO SAY THAT I BEGAN BEST BUY with a unique vision and a brilliant business plan, but I didn't. The truth is that I had no vision at all. I didn't even know what a business plan was. What I did have was ambition and a strong work ethic. And those traits, maybe above all others, have served me well over the years. Time and time again, I have seen the importance of not giving up, no matter what. Of not getting discouraged when things go wrong. Of not being dissuaded by people when they say that something can't be done.

I've learned there is always a way forward and, through unrelenting perseverance, you can find it—as I did, time and again, even in the early years of my life, long before I founded Best Buy.

It's important for me to talk about those pre–Best Buy years, because sometimes it seems to me that people think our company has always existed and it has always been big. That is hardly the case, of course. Best Buy didn't come into existence until 1983, when I was forty-two. I had already been in business for seventeen years with a company called Sound of Music.

Best Buy struggled. We did not start out with a beautiful, state-of-the-art headquarters building—we spent years in cramped offices where we had a lot of our business meetings in the hallways, bathrooms, and wherever we could find a space. We had very little cash in the bank—we faced down bankruptcy several times. We were hardly the leader in our industry—we had to fight off competitor after competitor (and sometimes supplier after supplier) just to stay alive. Even after we grew quite large, Wall Street often bet against us.

So the notion that we have always been big and successful kind of makes me want to laugh. But it also worries me, because when people get that idea, it's easy for them to assume that we will never *not* be big and successful. Nothing could be further from the truth. In fact, the bigger we get, the greater the danger is that we will forget just how tough it was to get where we are today. When that happens, a company can get complacent. People might shy away from big challenges. We might lose our capacity to struggle, to fight, to persist against all odds.

Believe me when I say that as tough as it was to become the $50 billion industry-leading company we are today, it's going to be even *tougher* to become the $150 billion global leader we need to become in the future in order to remain number one. The way we will make that happen—the way that any great accomplishment happens—is through perseverance: a dogged refusal to accept failure. I should know. After all, I came to a dead end in my very first full-time job much too soon. I had a wife and one child at the time, with another one on the way. And guess who my boss was, the guy who let me go?

My dad, Warren Schulze.

MY FAMILY OF HARD WORKERS

Before I tell you about the day Dad and I parted ways, let me talk a little bit about my background. I come from a hard-working family, and I have worked hard all my life. As I said in the Introduction, I started out as a paperboy at age eleven and, as I turn seventy, I'm still working hard every day. OK, I play golf a little more often than I used to, and I spend more time on my philanthropic and family activities, but I'm still very involved in the Best Buy business, as well as other businesses I own.

My origins are modest. My grandfather, Dad's father, was a bricklayer. He was a first-generation American who came here from Germany and settled his family in the Twin Cities area, ending up in a house on Sherburne Avenue in St. Paul. When I was a kid, I used to ride my bike over to visit him and Grandma on Saturday mornings after I finished my paper route. One time, Grandpa took me down to the basement to show me his workshop. I will never forget it. Everything was in perfect order. All the tools hung neatly, straight up and down, absolutely parallel. It made a big impression on me. Obviously, work was something that our family took very seriously.

My father must have inherited the trait from my grandfather, because he was also very big on being orderly. Sometimes he took it to an extreme. For example, he was extremely picky about how the Christmas tree should be decorated. The tinsel had to be hung perfectly perpendicular, with exactly one finger width between each strand. Large ornaments had to fill the spaces between branches, but no space should be too big. If it was, you had to fill in the gap. How? Dad was prepared for that. He always picked up a few extra pine boughs when he bought the tree. All you had to do was drill a hole in the trunk in the spot where the additional branch was needed. Whittle down the end of the new branch so it could be neatly and snugly inserted in the hole. *Voilà!* A nice, bushy, symmetrical tree.

Like father, like son—in that respect at least. I always kept my bedroom in good order. I made the bed before I left for school and picked up my clothes in the evening. Nothing ever was left lying around. The room was always spotless. When my two younger brothers came along, we shared the bedroom, and it was my job to teach them to pick up after themselves.

My mother with my sister, Judie, and me.

My mother was a hard worker, too. She was born Angela Lenarz, the youngest of eight children, and was brought up on a farm in Albany, a small town about eighty-five miles northwest of Minneapolis. She moved to the city as a young woman and found a job as a house-keeper for a wealthy family in the Highland Park area of St. Paul. She worked evenings as a hatcheck girl at the Prom Ballroom on University Avenue, and that's where she and my father met. They dated and got married in 1939.

Unlike my father, who devoted his life to work and was a pretty strict guy and a disciplinarian, Mom was a very warm and giving person. She loved to dance and sing. She loved spending time with her kids. She was a wonderful homemaker and cook and a caring member of the community. If a neighbor was sick or there was a function at church, Mom was always there with a hot meal.

Dad and I.

Saturday was a special day at our house because it was baking day, year-round. Mom and my sister, Judie, would bake bread, rolls, cakes, cupcakes, and—my favorite—oatmeal raisin cookies. While they were inside kneading the dough or mixing up the batter, I'd be outside taking care of my chores. There was always work to be done around the house, whether it was cutting the grass or shoveling snow, cleaning the windows or washing my Dad's car. When I was finished, I'd come inside to that fabulous aroma of freshly baked goodies.

In addition to being so engaged with life, Mom was also extremely well organized and efficient. She looked after everything and made sure that we dotted every *i* and crossed every *t*. She stressed, in particular, the importance of sending thank-you notes after we had visited somebody's home or when someone had done something nice for us. She thought it was very important to acknowledge people for the good things they did. That was Mom. I have never forgotten her lesson and have always made it a point to thank people, either with a note or directly in conversation, when they have done something valuable—whether in my personal life or at the company.

Now, I don't want to make it sound as though Dad was all work and no play. Two things I remember vividly demonstrate Dad's more relaxed side. Every summer the whole family would take a week's vacation on a lake, a different one each year, in either Minnesota or Wisconsin. There my dad taught me how to fish. He was also an avid reader, always interested in new ideas and information, and he enjoyed sharing newfound knowledge with his kids. I paid close attention to him and came to understand the importance of reading and constant learning.

Mostly, however, Dad spent his hours working so he could earn enough money to support his family, which eventually came to number four children. I followed his example. I worked my way through high school and, as a result, never had much time for after-school sports or for just hanging out with friends.

I TRY INNOVATION AT RED OWL

My first real job was in retail with the Red Owl grocery store chain. In my junior year of high school, I decided I needed to make more money than I could from my paper route. I applied for a job at the local Red Owl and was hired. I began as a carryout boy. My responsibilities were to greet customers as they came out of the checkout line, thank them for their business, and offer to carry their bags of groceries out to their car. I enjoyed meeting lots of people and having a chance to chat with them and get to know them a bit. I remembered what I had learned about customer service on my paper route and always placed the bags carefully into the customer's trunk. I was happy when my efforts were rewarded with a tip.

Soon I was promoted to a stocking position, and this was a whole different kettle of fish. My responsibility was to make sure that the shelves were filled with the necessary products to prepare for the evening rush. This work required some pretty heavy lifting; I had to unload cases and cartons of canned and packaged goods from the delivery truck, load up the pallets, push them out onto the floor, and then shift the products onto the shelves. I was in good physical condition, so the labor didn't bother me. Besides, I was making 75 cents more per hour than I had as a carryout boy, and I liked that.

What was much more challenging about the stock job was figuring out the best way to stage the pallets. In what order should I stack up the products? How many cartons of each? Was it more efficient to fill up a pallet with one or two products and fill the shelves completely? Or did it make more sense to pile on many different products and get a few of each onto the shelves so we wouldn't run out of anything?

I spent a lot of time thinking about that problem. I didn't know it at the time, but the consideration of how physical work is accomplished is the basis of the business theory known as "scientific management." It's all about finding the most efficient use of time and labor, and that's exactly what I was trying to figure out at the age of sixteen. The principles still apply today, and at Best Buy, we're always looking for better ways to configure our supply chain, stock our shelves, and manage work in the stores.

At Red Owl, I came to the conclusion that our staging process was highly inefficient. I was convinced that if we loaded up the pallets differently, we could restock the shelves much faster. I went to my boss, the store manager, and explained my plan to him. He wasn't interested. In fact, he was downright annoyed.

"That's none of your business," the manager told me. "Just get the product off the truck and put it where it belongs."

"But . . . ," I protested.

"Just do it," he snapped.

I went back to work, but I didn't give up on my idea. Maybe it was the image of Grandpa's tools or Mom's tidy kitchen or Dad's strands of tinsel or my own paper route process, but I really couldn't stand doing the work in such a sloppy and inefficient way. A couple of days later, I went again to the store manager and explained more about what I was thinking. Again he said no and told me to go back to work. Still, I wouldn't give up. I kept after him. One day, I guess I pushed it a little too hard.

"Listen, son," my boss said at last, "if you don't want to do it the way you're told, you're free to leave at any time." He stared at me, hands on his hips.

I thought about the steady work, about the good pay, about all the things I wanted to buy, about the money Dad expected me to contribute to the running of the family household. I thought about these things, and I made my decision.

"Good-bye," I said to the store manager as I untied my apron strings. "Thanks." I shook his hand and handed him the apron. "And good luck."

I walked out of the store in a state of shock. *What just happened?* I thought. I had quit a well-paying job because I disagreed with the store manager about how to stock the shelves. *What happens next?*

I learned two things from my experience at Red Owl. The first was about innovation. I had naturally assumed that my manager would be interested in hearing about new and better ways to get our work done. Wrong. Not only was he not interested, he did not think it was my place to question him or make suggestions. I was a lowly stock boy. He was the boss. I couldn't tolerate that then, and I still can't today. New ideas can, and often do, come from anyone, in any part of the company. It's through good ideas from people throughout the organization that Best Buy has grown while other companies have fallen by the wayside.

The second lesson was about risk. I discovered that sometimes you have to be willing to put it all on the line and to accept the consequences of taking a stand. My friends couldn't believe what I had done. They said, *You quit? You ditched a perfectly good job because you didn't like the way they were putting cans on the shelf? Are you nuts?* But I didn't think I was nuts. I knew I was a good worker. I knew I could get another job. I knew I could tolerate a bit of uncertainty until I found a new position. What I couldn't accept was that a manager would deliberately ignore a good idea.

It happens, I know. At Best Buy, we want to hear about new ideas, and we encourage people to share them. But I'm sure we have ignored good ideas in our history, and we probably still do so today. Sometimes there are good reasons for it. Especially in a big company like ours, there are so many ideas floating around that they can just get lost or swallowed up. But a manager should never *deliberately* ignore an idea. And even if the idea doesn't get accepted or can't be implemented, the person who came up with it should be respected, thanked, and informed about what's going on with his or her suggestion, and why it might have been rejected.

You can be sure that if someone makes a good suggestion and it's completely ignored the first time, there won't be a second time. That's how innovation gets suppressed, and that's how companies fall behind.

WHY I DIDN'T GO TO COLLEGE

I was right about my prospects. After I quit Red Owl, it didn't take me long to get another job. I was hired by Montgomery Ward, one of America's greatest retail chains at the time—right up there with

Sears and J. C. Penney. It was quite a step up from the Red Owl grocery chain. Headquartered in Chicago, Montgomery Ward operated
department stores around the country and also had a huge mail-
order business, dealing mostly in home goods.

I worked at the massive distribution center at 1400 University
Avenue in St. Paul. I'd drive the Green Hornet to the building right
after school, punch in at 4:00 P.M., and finish up at 11:00 P.M. My
job was to sort through the packages that were ready for customer
delivery, grouping them by zip code so they'd be ready for pickup by
the truck drivers the following morning. Sometimes I worked alone,
sometimes with one or two others, sorting through thousands of
packages during the seven-hour shift.

Unlike Red Owl, I thought Montgomery Ward had a pretty
efficient process. The only problem with the job was that it was
extremely boring. Package after package after package. Zip code after
zip code after zip code. Very little human interaction. No customers.
No chance for tips. Not really any opportunity for learning. It was all
about accuracy and avoiding mistakes. The best thing about the job
was the pay, $1.80 an hour, so I stuck with it for almost a year. I just
wanted to make as much money as I could before I graduated from
high school.

My plan was to get a higher education. I was accepted at the
College of St. Thomas and I intended to start classes in September
1958. I was eager to learn all I could and make the most of myself,
and I was looking forward to my four years as a serious student. But
there was a complication. At the time, the U.S. military had a draft
system and could call up young men to serve in the Armed Services.
The most famous draftee of the time was Elvis Presley, who had been
conscripted in 1957 and spent two years in the Army.

The country was at peace in 1958, though, and young men could
get a deferment so they could attend college. Still, the way for me

to have the most control in the long run over my service require-
ment was to enroll in the Air National Guard, which required a six-
month training period followed by weekend service over a period
of six years—rather than the two-year commitment of regular service. So that's what I signed up for. I arranged to attend an initial
three-month period of basic training at Lackland Air Force Base
in San Antonio, Texas, which I would do in the summer, so I could
come back to Minnesota in time to start school in September. I
would then take a semester away from school to do a second three-
month stint of technical training starting in January. Then I would
become a "weekend warrior," spending one weekend each month in
refresher training. I would also be on call to serve during an emergency, if necessary.

Sergeant Schulze.

Well, the Air National Guard didn't seem to be too much better at organizing things than Red Owl had been. I went down to Texas, but boot camp got delayed, and then it was extended. So by the time I got back to Minneapolis, classes at the College of St. Thomas were already well under way, and it was too late to join in. Then I was told that my technical training would not start in January but would be pushed back to the following summer instead. I decided I'd better get a job while I was waiting to fulfill my service obligation.

At the time, Dad was working as a manufacturer's rep, selling electronics components—fuses, semiconductors, transistors, controls, and the like—to big industrial companies such as Honeywell and 3M. He also represented some consumer electronics equipment, mostly TV components. One of the companies he called on was Schaak Electronics, whose owner, Lee Schaak, was at the time a customer and friend of his. Dad told Lee that I was looking for a short-term opportunity to fill in the gap before I had to report to my tech training. Lee knew I had experience with retail, that I understood customers, and that I had a grasp on the ins and outs of stocking a store, so he hired me to work the counter in his shop and to stock the shelves. That's where I got my first taste of the electronics business and learned a lot about dealing with suppliers and big industrial customers.

The following summer, I bid farewell to Schaak as planned and reported for duty at Lowry Air Force Base in Denver, Colorado. There I spent six months learning even more about electronics-related issues, mostly missile technology and air traffic control. By the time I got done with my training, however, it was well into the fall semester of 1959. I was a whole year behind already, and I felt pretty out of sync with the college track.

As I was trying to decide what to do next, Dad suggested that I come to work with him. He said that we could split the business in two. He'd continue with the industrial components part of the business,

THE EARLY DAYS / 33

and I could try to build up the consumer electronics side, which was still very small in terms of sales. I said fine, I'd give it a try.

and I could try to build up the consumer electronics side, which was still very small in terms of sales. I said fine, I'd give it a try.

We repped several consumer brands at the time, and one of them was Sony. The company had just one major product then, a seven-inch reel-to-reel audio tape recorder that sold for $129. You've never seen or heard of such a thing? It worked with quarter-inch magnetic audio tape, chocolate brown in color, that came on a plastic reel. You'd pull the tape from the full reel and thread it through the recording heads and onto a take-up reel. It recorded in monaural sound only, not stereo. Even so, it was an exciting technology, and people who bought the system thought of themselves as advanced and knowledgeable audiophiles.

Pretty soon I was calling on consumer electronics dealers throughout a five-state area: Wisconsin, North and South Dakota, Iowa, and Minnesota. I was meeting lots of new people, involved in a rapidly growing industry, and building a business. Everything was great. I felt that I was truly in control of my own destiny.

The idea of college, while still very attractive to me (as it still is today), began to fade. After all, I was making money and building a business! That seemed much more exciting to me than the prospect of college. What's more, there was something else very important going on in my life at the time. Her name was Sandy.

SANDY AND I GET TOGETHER

To introduce you to the woman who became my wife of nearly forty years, I'll have to back up for a moment.

During my senior year of high school, my sister, Judie, worked at Kings Pharmacy, a drugstore just a block from our house. One day, I stopped in to say hi and found there was another young woman in the store. Judie introduced me to her friend, Sandy Larkin.

Sandy.

Sandy was nice and friendly, and we got to talking. Although her family was originally from the Twin Cities, they had moved to Kansas City when she was a child so she had spent most of her early life there. As a result, she spoke with a beautiful Southern lilt in her voice that I found captivating. She told me all about herself. Her family had recently returned to Minneapolis from Kansas City because her father, an executive with a chemical firm, had been transferred.

Sandy was looking forward to starting school at St. Catherine's College, just a few blocks away. She was the oldest of four kids in the family. I told Sandy that even though I was actually born about three minutes after my twin sister, I always *felt* as though I were the oldest. I explained that I was in the electronics business and planned to attend the College of St. Thomas in the fall, but that I would be spending the summer at boot camp in Texas.

We hit it off. I asked Sandy for her address so I could write her while I was away, and I gave her my address in Texas. I didn't know if anything would come of it or if she'd actually write me. But the first week I was there, sure enough, a letter arrived. I received one from her every week for the thirteen weeks of boot camp.

When I came back to Minneapolis, Sandy and I started seeing each other pretty regularly. We'd go to a movie. I'd go over to her family's house, or she'd come over to ours. I was working at Schaak Electronics; she was in college. We grew very close. That summer, while I was at my tech training in Denver, Sandy kept the correspondence going. In fact, she wrote me a letter every *day*, not every week, for the entire five months I was there.

In her letters, Sandy told me about school and how she wasn't happy at St. Catherine's and was thinking about transferring to the University of Minnesota (eventually, she did). I wrote about what I was studying in tech school and how I was hoping to get back to Minneapolis by Christmas. We talked about everything and any-

Sandy and me
(with a full head of hair).

thing in those letters, and they brought us even closer together. You can cover a lot of territory in the space of 150 letters—talk about persever-ance! I still have them, and I treasure every one.

I did get home for Christmas of 1960. Sandy and I picked up where we had left off. Soon enough we got engaged, and we were married in June 1962.

Sandy proved to be the most wonderful and amazing partner— for me personally, as a mother to our four kids, and as an incredible booster of the Best Buy business. Without Sandy, and her unflagging support of me and her participation in every aspect of our operation, Best Buy would not be the company it is today.

I FIND A NEW PURPOSE

OK, now let's get to the punch line: the day Dad and I parted company.

Things had been going really well, I thought. Sandy and I bought a little house in West St. Paul, a suburban neighborhood that is actually *east* of the city. We bought the house for $13,400, which seemed like a lot of money at the time. It had three bedrooms and a garage tucked under, big enough for our growing family—Sandy, me, our daughter Susan, and a second baby on the way. The mortgage payment was $129 a month. Our utilities cost more than that then!

The business, too, was doing well. We had a small office in Bloomington, a suburb to the south of downtown Minneapolis. There were just four of us: Dad, me, a part-time salesperson who worked with Dad, and a receptionist who did the administrative work.

I was on the road most of the time, calling on more and more dealers throughout my five-state territory. I was gradually building up a portfolio of electronics products aimed at an interesting consumer group: music lovers, audiophiles, and technology enthusiasts with enough affluence to purchase the latest and greatest

Dad (center) and me with Bud Fields, one of our suppliers.

advances in audio equipment as they arrived. We kept adding new lines: Sherwood amplifiers and tuners; Shure Brothers microphones and phonograph cartridges; Garrard record changers; Wharfedale speakers, a high-end line made in England. During that period the technology was gradually moving from monaural to stereo sound, and later, from vacuum tubes to transistors.

Not only was I the chief salesperson for the consumer business, but it seemed like I did virtually everything else, too. I designed ad campaigns. I conducted training sessions for the retail salespeople. I'd visit stores on Saturdays and help out. I enjoyed seeing the outcome of my work—consumers buying the products I had made available to the retailer and walking out of the store with smiles on their faces. I realized that we were not really in the electronics business at all. We were selling entertainment.

I was having a lot of fun, and it was paying off. In fact, after my fourth year in the business, my consumer electronics "division" was outperforming the industrial piece that Dad ran. I felt pretty good about that. Good enough that it seemed like a reasonable time to ask for a raise. With a new house and a growing family, Sandy and I certainly could use the money.

Dad was on the road most of the week, too, so he always went into the office on Saturday morning to catch up on his paperwork. I figured that would be the best time to have the money discussion with him. So that fateful Saturday morning, I told Sandy that I was going down to the office to talk with my dad.

"What about?" she asked.

"Well, I've accomplished a lot in the years we've worked together," I said, rehearsing what I was going to say. "I think it's time for a change."

I remember that meeting vividly. As soon as I got to the office, I asked Dad if I could speak with him. We often talked on Saturdays, usually about a road trip I was planning, a new promotion, or a new line of equipment I was considering. He said "sure." He clearly didn't anticipate what the topic was going to be.

I started off a little tentatively. "Well, Dad, as you know, we have one little girl and we're looking forward to having another child. I think it's time that we talk about my responsibility with the firm. How we're structured. And . . . umm . . . my compensation."

Pause.

Dad looked at me strangely. "Compensation?"

"Yes. I would like a raise."

"You don't think you're well paid enough now?"

Now I was into it, and I could see it wasn't going to be as easy as I had hoped. "Candidly, Dad, I'm willing to accept that what I've earned has been fair thus far. But I think I've proved what I can do. You know, we've been able to generate pretty good sales figures."

That was an understatement. He knew very well that the consumer sales business was bringing in more revenue than the industrial side.

"And what with two children and school costs and everything," I continued, "I really need to earn some more money."

I could see Dad stiffening up a little.

"Well, son," he said, "I don't know that you're ready for a raise."

Now I felt myself getting a little hot under the collar. "You may not know that I'm ready, Dad," I replied, "but I think I deserve another seventy-five dollars a week." I was making $1,200 a month then and thought I deserved at least $1,500.

"Seventy-five more a week!" Dad was turning red. "I don't think you've demonstrated that you've learned enough about the business to justify *that* kind of income."

I knew Dad well, and I could see that his mind was made up. "OK, Dad," I said, starting to back away. "OK. Thanks. I understand. Now I know where you sit. So be it."

"Let's revisit this a year from now," he said, softening a little. "We'll see how you do. Then maybe we can talk about a raise."

I didn't say anything. I just left the office, got in my car, and drove home.

"How'd it go?" Sandy asked.

"It's over," I said. "I'm leaving. I'm going to start my own business."

Sandy was surprised—maybe even a little shocked. "You're going to leave your father?"

"I left him already," I said. "He doesn't appreciate what I'm doing. He's stuck in his own ideas. He's telling me what he thinks. He's not listening to what I'm saying."

Sandy studied me. She knew that Dad and I were alike in one way: once our minds were made up, there was no going back.

"But Dick, are you sure . . . ?"

"Sandy," I said, "I need to be in control of my own destiny. You know that."

Sandy did know that, and she supported me. Although we talked some more, we both realized that the die had been cast.

In one way, it was too bad. I had expected to take over the business from my father one day, and now I felt disappointed that I wouldn't and hurt that he didn't value my contribution as much as I thought he should. In another way, the split was probably inevitable. Dad had to be careful about costs, especially the salaries he paid. Our company was essentially at the mercy of our suppliers. They could cancel a rep's contract with thirty days' notice, without cause, and often they would do so. What's more, reps were paid a percentage of the sales volume they did—usually 5 percent. But as the rep's volume increased, the percentage went down. You might find yourself earning 1 percent or 2 percent on high-volume lines. So if Dad increased my salary and we lost an important line or our percentage went down, it could put a serious squeeze on profits.

I thought about all of that over the weekend, and it just strengthened my resolve. Even if my dad agreed to a raise next year, the
amount I could earn would be limited. The only way to control my
own destiny and earn the kind of money I wanted was to go my own
way. So, that Monday morning, I went down to the office.

"Dad," I said, "I've decided to leave the company."

He was stunned. He did not expect that at all.

"I'm giving my two weeks' notice," I said.

And that was that.

When my mother found out, she was upside down with my
father. "This is the worst possible thing you could ever do to your
son! How could you treat him like this?"

Dad replied that I needed more experience before he could justify a higher salary. This did not convince my mother, and she never
really forgave Dad for it. I don't know if that incident drove a wedge
between the two of them, but their relationship was never quite the
same afterwards.

That was the second time I quit a job—and it was the last. Both
times I left because I came up against a manager (one of whom,
unfortunately, was my father) who wouldn't listen to ideas about
how to improve the business and wouldn't accept that things had to
change. I knew in my bones that you couldn't run a company that
way for very long. I was right: Dad was out of business within a few
years. (He came to work for us.) And although Red Owl got pretty
big in the Midwest, with 441 stores at its peak, the company eventually sold out to Supervalu.

Now, I know it might sound as if I'm being a bit harsh on Dad.
Admittedly, it was sometimes difficult for me to appreciate his strong
points when I was a young man. But as my life has evolved, I have
realized how blessed I was to have had a father who was so focused
on getting things done properly, getting them done on time, and

always making sure that I knew how to do a job and do it well. We didn't see eye to eye when it came to the business, but that doesn't mean I don't appreciate my father and what he taught me.

So there I was, with a family and a mortgage, and without a job or a business. I had to figure out what to do next—and fast. I took stock of my assets. First and foremost, I had a wonderful wife who was willing to support me and work alongside me to build our lives and our business. I had developed some strong and lasting relationships with the manufacturers we represented. I had gained a lot of knowledge. I knew a good deal about the consumer electronics business and about the suppliers who created the products. I had gotten lots of valuable experience and learned that I was good at the business. I could help customers pick products. I knew how to display and demonstrate them. I could train salespeople. I understood advertising and promotion. I could manage costs and turn a profit.

In other words, I knew what I enjoyed the most and where I wanted to go: retail. So, in those early years of work, I had discovered my *passion*. I had also demonstrated the *perseverance* to achieve whatever I set my sights on. Now I just had to define my *purpose*, and I did so soon enough . . . when I started my own retail business.

As it turned out, that would be my destiny.

CHAPTER TWO

SOUND OF MUSIC

*It Can Take a Long Time
to Build a Business,
and It Can Fall Apart Fast*

I WOULD LIKE TO BE ABLE TO SAY THAT, BACK IN 1966, I knew exactly how to start and run a retail business. But I didn't. Maybe that's why it took so long to build my first company, Sound of Music. And maybe that's why, thirteen years later, I nearly lost the whole thing.

When I started out, I certainly did not expect that it would all come down to a fateful meeting at the Decathlon Club in Bloomington, Minnesota, not far from our headquarters at the time. During that five-hour meeting in 1979, we did what I thought we would never do: we prepared bankruptcy papers for the company I had founded and nurtured for so many years. As successful as the company had been, both the overall retailing climate and the consumer electronics industry in particular had changed dramatically. New federal regulations had made it easier to sell goods across state lines, which meant we were competing with mail-order houses and national chains. What's more, our agreements with manufacturers obligated us to service their products even if the customer had purchased them through some other channel. We ended up doing a lot repairs for little or no profit. Very quickly, it seemed, everything had closed in on us. We were out of cash, out of credit, and out of time.

I came *this close* to signing those papers. If I had, within a week Sound of Music would have been history, and Best Buy might never have existed.

But I'm getting ahead of myself. Before I tell you about that meeting, let me explain how we got there. Current Best Buy employees may not even know there was a predecessor company called Sound of Music, what kind of business it was, or that it nearly went under. Well, as I said before, Best Buy was not always big. We did not always have cash in the bank. And we were hardly an overnight success.

It's important to look back and remember how quickly every-thing can unravel, especially as we look ahead to a whole new era of electronics retailing, in which our business is much more global than ever before and engaged as much online as it is in physical stores.

In other words, what happened to us in 1979 *could happen again.*

THE SOUND OF WHAT?

Starting a business in 1966 was very different than it is now.

This was before the age of the hot technology start-ups like Amazon and Google that we're so familiar with today. Young people didn't dream of becoming entrepreneurs. There weren't billions of dollars in investment capital available. You didn't start a business hoping you could sell your company or go public in five or ten years and retire at the age of forty.

Most people who wanted to create a new business back in those days did it the old-fashioned way: we started small and expected to stick with the company for a long time. Many of us opened up shop "on a shoestring"—meaning that we invested almost nothing and got by on cash flow from the very beginning. If we needed capital, we dipped into our own savings, borrowed from our families and friends, got a bank loan, or arranged credit terms with our suppliers.

If you didn't have any savings or couldn't get enough credit, you could do what I did: mortgage your house. That was the biggest asset I had and the only way I could raise enough money to open my very first retail store.

I remember talking with Sandy about the idea. "I'm putting it all on the line, Sandy," I said. "The whole enchilada." That sounds a little dramatic now, but that's how it felt at the time. Once again, I was contemplating a big risk, just as I had when I quit the Red Owl grocery store. Only much more so.

"Dick, you're only twenty-six," Sandy said. "You're not an old man. You've learned a lot already. You'll always land on your feet."

So, with Sandy's support, I went to the bank and they gave me a second mortgage—all of $9,000. Sandy's father, Bob Larkin, who was a successful businessman, also invested a bit of money.

What was my business plan? Such as it was, the plan was to build on the knowledge of the consumer electronics business that I had gained by working with Dad and by calling on all those suppliers and retailers. Unlike our competitors, such as Schaak Electronics, we would sell records and sheet music as "traffic builders." In other words, although we wouldn't make much profit on the music products, they would attract customers and bring them into our stores. That would enable us to sell more audio components and other electronics hardware, which were our core business.

As I was considering exactly where to open our first store and what to call it, I connected with a former high school classmate named Gary Smoliak. I hadn't been close friends with him, but he knew a lot about music and was interested in opening a store, too, so we decided to go into business together.

Gary and I were complete opposites. I was the serious, nose-to-the-grindstone young man with the wife, the kids, and a mortgage. Gary was a "greaser," complete with leather jacket, slicked-back hair, and a zest for having a good time. He loved music. He knew all about audio equipment. And he couldn't get enough of hanging out with other music lovers and audiophiles.

Gary believed that the natural market for our business was college kids, ages eighteen to twenty-five. The mid-1960s were an incredible time for music, especially on campuses across the country. The Beatles were at the peak of their popularity, as were Bob Dylan and other folkies; rock 'n' roll bands like Pink Floyd and Fleetwood Mac were just getting started. College kids were crazy about records and tapes. They wanted music everywhere, and they liked it loud, clean, and clear. They bought record players so they could spin the latest albums; they bought tape recorders to copy and share the albums, as well as to record their own music. Remember, there were no CD players or iPods back then—not even cassette players.

Gary and I brought different skills to the partnership. Gary would be the music expert, and I would handle the business side of things. The fact is that I liked music, but I wasn't crazy about it the way Gary and the college kids were. Actually, music was kind of a sore point with me, at least in part because of an incident that took place way back in the third grade.

There I was, eight years old, sitting in the front row of music class next to a friend named Jack Mathes. All the kids were singing a song together, and Jack and I were really getting into it. We got louder and louder, and the teacher kept shooting us dirty looks. Finally she held up her hand, and everybody stopped. She glared at me, then at Jack.

"You boys are terrible singers," she said. "Either you need to go sit in the back row or you need to just *keep your mouths shut* while the rest of the children sing properly."

Wow. As you can imagine, we both felt demeaned and embarrassed, and even today I'm still not much on singing because of it. But one very special thing came of that episode: Jack and I became fast friends and, some years later, our families did, too. Jack and I had a great friendship that lasted sixty-two years, until he lost his battle with pulmonary fibrosis in 2011.

So, I had a business partner in Gary, a few thousand dollars in capital to get us going, and what could loosely be called a business plan. All we needed now was a name and a place. Gary and I kicked around a few names and settled on Sound of the Northwest. We liked it because it was different from the other music stores in the area. It didn't have the word *electronics* in it, unlike our two biggest competitors: Schaak Electronics, where I had worked that spring before going off to technical training in the Air National Guard, and Team Electronics, a franchise chain. Remember, we thought of ourselves as being in the *entertainment* business, and to us that was very different from the electronics business, which sounded industrial and old-fashioned.

Well, the name didn't fly. When I went to register Sound of the Northwest with the state government, I was told we couldn't use it because it was too close to the name of an existing company, Northwest Sound Service. We had to come up with something different.

At that time, in addition to folk and rock music, show tunes were also very popular, both on Broadway and in the movies. One of the biggest movie hits the previous year was *The Sound of Music*, starring Julie Andrews. It was based on the Broadway musical, and people loved the songs—"Edelweiss," "My Favorite Things," "Climb Ev'ry Mountain," and, of course, "The Sound of Music"—and were buying up the soundtrack like hotcakes. Gary and I thought Sound of Music was a catchy title and would be perfect for the store. So we borrowed it, created a logo, and that was that. If it had been today, the producers of the movie probably would have come after us for copyright infringement, but those were less litigious times. Besides, we were tiny and the movie studios weren't paying attention to us—yet.

One of the early Sound of Music stores.

Now all we needed was a space. We found a good one in St. Paul, about 1,200 square feet in size, at the corner of St. Clair Avenue and Hamline Avenue. It was just a few blocks away from four private colleges—St. Catherine, Macalester, St. Thomas, and Hamline University—with thousands of students in the area every day. It looked pretty appealing.

We opened that first Sound of Music store in August 1966. We sold audio components and records, guitars and sheet music. If it had anything to do with music, we carried it. We stocked brands like Sony, Sherwood, Dual, Acoustic Research, Bose, and Altec Lansing. We also had a one-man service department, run by Joe Bush. He was kept very busy fixing turntables and doing other repairs on his bench in the basement of the store.

It didn't take long for us to build a loyal clientele, and I began to think that this business had real growth potential. Being a pretty ambitious person, I wanted to open another store right away. I knew we didn't have the profits we needed or the capacity to borrow any more money, but I figured there had to be another way for us to buy the inventory and fixtures and to handle all the costs of getting a second store up and running.

Here's where the relationships I had cultivated while working as a manufacturer's rep with Dad paid off. During my days as a rep, I had called on lots of retailers in the Twin Cities area and had gotten to know the owners and the businesses pretty well. Two of them were obviously struggling. One of the owners had health issues, and the other operation was limping along financially. Both were at attractive store locations. Bergo Company was on Tenth Street in downtown Minneapolis. Kencraft Hi-Fi was in Dinkytown, a four-block area of shops and restaurants, right next to the campus of the University of Minnesota with all its fraternity and sorority houses. (Bob Dylan had lived in Dinkytown and was very involved in the local folk music scene until he moved from the Twin Cities to New York in 1961.)

I visited both of the store owners and asked, "Have you given any thought to selling your business?" They jumped at the chance. We couldn't buy their businesses outright, of course, but I figured we could pay them off gradually, from cash flow. To do that, however, we would need a little help from our equipment and music suppliers. I went to talk with them, one by one, and asked if they would be willing to help us buy out these businesses, both of which would probably fail otherwise, by extending our credit terms. They all said yes. Why not? It would be much better for them to have three healthy businesses in operation than to have two go belly up. The deals worked, and within four months of starting the company, we had three Sound of Music locations: downtown, Dinkytown, and the St. Paul college area.

We fell into a work rhythm. Gary chose the music and bought all the records and tapes, and I managed all the rest of the purchasing. I also did pretty much everything else. I trained our store managers, designed and set up displays, and figured out the floor plan. And as we grew in volume and revenue, I got more and more interested in the complexities and subtleties of running a company—inventory turns, return on investment, advertising, and the demographics of the people we served.

In our first partial year of operation as three stores, 1967, we grossed a total of $173,000. In our first full year, we reached $1,304,000 in revenue. Sounds like pretty small potatoes now, but not then. We were able to cover our expenses and pay our employees and suppliers, and I was able to take home what seemed like a fairly decent salary at the time. I certainly was doing better than I had as a factory rep. I was learning a lot, building relationships with customers and suppliers. The business was starting to grow.

A RIFT

However, as time went on, my relationship with Gary deteriorated. I realized that he and I had very different views on the business. He was in seventh heaven, hanging out in the stores, talking to customers (especially the young college women), listening to music, and tinkering with the equipment.

The music scene was just exploding. You had the Beatles and the Rolling Stones, Jimi Hendrix, Elvis, the Supremes, the Platters, Jefferson Airplane . . . The Doors appeared on the Ed Sullivan show and were subsequently banned from ever appearing again. The summer of 1967 was known as "the summer of love." Nearly one hundred thousand people gathered in the Haight-Ashbury neighborhood of San Francisco to celebrate freedom, youth culture, and the hippie movement—and to play a *lot* of music. Our Sound of Music stores benefited from all that.

Truth be told, during those days, Gary was probably having a little too much fun and not paying enough attention to the business. Although he was interested in building the company, he wanted to stick with the college market he loved so much, where he thought it was all happening. I wanted to do more in the suburbs, where I believed there was a much larger market with more diversified demographics.

Gary and I also disagreed about how to distribute the proceeds from the business. He wanted to pocket all the profit, while I believed we should take our earnings and invest them in building the business. Interestingly enough, Gary's father, Nate Smoliak, who was our bookkeeper at the time, sided with me on these issues. "You should keep investing in the future," he said.

As it turned out, Gary and I just couldn't come to an agreement, and we finally decided that one of us should buy out the other. It should not surprise those who know me to learn that I prevailed in that debate. I would become the sole owner of the company, and I didn't insist on a noncompete clause from Gary.

To seal the deal we needed a legal agreement, but we didn't have a lawyer at the time. Fortunately, Gary's father had done some work with a small general litigation firm in town called Robins, Davis, and Lyons. (It's still going strong as Robins, Kaplan, Miller, and Ciresi.) We set up an appointment with them and were introduced to a young lawyer named Elliot Kaplan. He was a Minnesota native who had earned his bachelor's degree in business administration at the University of Minnesota and his law degree at the University of Minnesota Law School. Little did we know that he had just been named an associate partner of his firm, the youngest ever to attain that position.

Here's how Elliot remembers our meeting:

"I got a call from one of our senior partners, who said, 'There are two young guys coming in to the office tomorrow. I know the father of one of them. His kid has a partner and they have a stereo store or two here in town, and they want to break up their partnership. Can you handle that?' I said yes. But I'd never done one of these before, so I figured it out overnight and I was ready for them when they came in the next day.

I knew Gary Smoliak because he lived in my neighborhood. Then there was this other fellow by the name of Dick Schulze, whom I didn't know. I prepared the partnership dissolution document, so each one could go his own way. They were both planning to remain in the business and potentially would be competitors.

At the conclusion of the meeting, Gary said to me, 'Now, I'd like you to represent me going forward.' And Dick said, 'You know, I'd like you to do the same for me.' I said, 'Guys, I'd feel better if I represented only one of you. You're going to be competitors, and it's just easier that way. There could be conflicts of interest.' Gary said, 'Remember, my dad does business here and I know you. You should represent me.' I said, 'OK, let me think about it overnight.' So I thought about it that evening and made a decision in the morning. I picked up the telephone and called Dick Schulze. I said, 'Dick, I'm going to represent you.' He said, 'Great.' Then I called Gary and said, 'I have decided to represent Dick.' Gary didn't ask me why.

Why did I choose Dick? There was something about him that just stood out. His ethics, his values, and his commitment to the business. He was very straightforward. He tried

*to be very fair in the trans-
action, whereas Gary focused
on getting the better deal for
himself. And so that was the
beginning of my relation-
ship with Dick."*

*Eloise and Elliot Kaplan
in recent years.*

I felt the same way about
Elliot. I could see that he was
a fair, honest, straightforward
guy with strong values. His firm
became the legal counsel for the
company, and eventually Elliot
joined our board of directors. He
retired from the Best Buy board in 2011, after forty years of wonderful contribution and valued service to the company.

As for Gary, after we split, he opened a competing store right
across the street from Sound of Music in Dinkytown. It was a bit of
a thorn in our side at first, but it went out of business in a couple of
years. Next Gary opened a bike shop, but that failed, too. He passed
away in 2008.

GOING PUBLIC

In 1969, three years after our founding, it became clear there was
sufficient demand for music and stereo equipment that we could
open more stores beyond the original three. But we still didn't have
any capital to speak of, and we couldn't fund any more new stores
from cash flow or extended credit terms, so we decided to take a
chance on going public. That is, we would raise capital by offering
shares of stock in the company.

This sounds pretty grand, but I'm not talking about the kind of huge public offering that has become so well known over recent decades. We weren't going to offer millions of shares and list Sound of Music on the New York Stock Exchange or any other public exchange. (That came later.) We were going for what is known as a local "over the counter" sale, which simply means that the offering is managed by an underwriter who deals directly with a fairly small number of customers. The offering is not listed and is not regulated the same way as is an initial public offering (IPO) of a company like Google or Microsoft.

Going public is an important milestone in the life of any company, but I really had no idea how to go about it. So we did it the same way we did everything else back then—cautiously, even a little bit warily, making sure we really understood what we were getting into. And we relied on Elliot Kaplan to negotiate the deal with the underwriter.

Of course Elliot didn't know what he was doing either. He had never done a public offering. But he got advice from other lawyers in his firm and put together a good plan. We visited a number of underwriters in the Twin Cities area. They all said, "We don't know if we can sell this, but we'll work with you on a 'best efforts' basis." In a best-efforts deal, the underwriter agrees to do his best to sell the entire offering—but if he can't, he has no obligation to pick up the remaining shares.

Elliot was not going for it. He said, "No. We're not going to do that. We have to have a firm underwriting." A "firm underwriting" means that the underwriter guarantees that the total number of shares will be sold, and if they aren't, the underwriter will buy the outstanding ones.

Finally, we found a local underwriter by the name of Schopf and Long that agreed to do a firm underwriting. We settled on an offering of one hundred thousand shares at $3.30 each, with the underwriter receiving 30 cents per share as commission. We thought that sounded pretty terrific.

Well, it wasn't quite as terrific as we thought. The shares went on the market and started to sell, but slowly, and mostly to people we knew or those who had some stake in the business. Elliot bought some. His mother bought some. Some of my friends and family bought shares. After a couple of weeks, the underwriter came to us and said, "I think we can sell sixty thousand shares, tops." So that meant there would remain about forty thousand shares that would go begging.

Here's where Elliot really proved his toughness. He said to the underwriter, "I don't care if you can't sell them. You guaranteed the sale. Why don't you just write a check to us for a hundred thousand dollars?"

The underwriter said that he didn't have $100,000.

Elliot said, "You have a bank, don't you?"

The underwriter said yes, he worked with First National Bank (now U.S. Bank).

Elliot looked at the underwriter as if to say, *Well, get moving.*

And he did. The underwriter borrowed $100,000 from First National and, as collateral, gave the bank the remaining shares in Sound of Music. So we got our $300,000, which seemed like a huge amount of money at the time, and it was enough to get us going on our expansion plans.

Now we were a publicly held company, allowed to sell stock in the state of Minnesota, and we soon learned that going public has its upside and its downside. (It still does.) One of the most obvious downsides is that the stock sometimes drops in value. That's exactly what our stock did a year after the offering: it dropped to 60 cents per share. But that turned out to be an upside for us, because First National Bank called me and said, "Dick, we're not in the business of owning your stock. Would you buy it from us for sixty or seventy cents a share?"

Elliot and I talked it over. Did we want to invest that much money in ourselves? We finally decided we did. I managed to come up with the money, and we did our first buyback.

I should add that Schopf and Long, the underwriter, did not last. Two or three years after our offering, they were gone. Not too surprising, given the deal they had made with us!

Back then, I was beginning to realize what everybody else seemed to know already: most small businesses like ours don't last very long. The strain of unpredictable cash flow, all-too-predictable supplier payments, lack of borrowing capacity, inventory shrink, employee turnover, and all the rest makes it very difficult for a small business to survive more than a few years. Most don't.

We did. Not because we were so much smarter than anybody else. Not because our stores were so much different from any of the others. We survived because of the *perseverance* I've talked about, because of our *passion* for the business, and because of our belief in our *purpose*. And there has been another very important factor, as well: the amazing people we were able to attract.

Elliot was certainly one of them. Already he had proved to be a tough negotiator on our behalf. But as I said, he could also be incredibly generous to the point of being softhearted. A lawyer, softhearted? Well, after the IPO, Sound of Music continued to do business with Elliot's firm of Robins, Davis, and Lyons. The firm handled leases, regulatory issues, and personnel contracts for us, and billed us $200 to $300 a month—not a lot of money, but it was steady, and we were building a good, strong relationship.

After a few months, Elliot came to me and suggested that we put his firm on a retainer of $500 a month. He said, "If I spend more time than that, you benefit. If I spend less, I benefit. It all evens out."

That's what we did for about a year. In late 1969, however, our cash flow got a little tight, and the retainer was starting to feel like an extravagance we couldn't afford. I called Elliot and said, "We're having a hard time paying our bills. I just can't pay you the retainer right now. If you want to fire me, go ahead and fire me."

He said, "Dick, don't worry about it. I'm going to do something I don't have the authority to do, because I'm not the managing partner in the firm. Here's what I'll do: I won't send you any invoices until you tell me you can pay them. In the meantime, I will keep working with you and do whatever you need. Just let me know when you're ready for the invoices again."

About six months later, we got over the hump. I called Elliot and said, "Elliot, I think we can pay you now. In fact, let's take it up to a thousand a month."

Not long after that, I invited Elliot to join our board. It was a small board—just me; Sandy's father, Bob Larkin; Joe Francis, founder of the Barbers Hairstyling Salon (which later became Great Clips); and now Elliot. Over time, Elliot and I became friends and then our families became friends. The Kaplans had young kids, about the same ages as our kids. We spent some wonderful times together.

Elliot was an important early member of the Sound of Music family, but he wasn't the only one who joined us near the start and helped shape the company as it grew. One of the most important of these was a former seminary student, a guy whose father had wanted him to be a pastor. His name was Bradbury Anderson, a.k.a. Brad.

BRAD, THE PASTOR'S SON, LEARNS RETAIL

One of the amazing things about our business, both then and now, is that it gives people a great opportunity to invent and reinvent themselves. When I talk with employees who have been with Best Buy for some time, I hear many of them say the same thing: "Dick, you know, I never imagined that I could accomplish what I have with Best Buy. If you told me that I'd be where I am now, doing what I'm doing, I wouldn't have believed it." Store managers tell me that all the time. Home office staff members say the same thing. Brian Dunn, our current CEO, has said that to me. And so has Brad Anderson.

Of course, with Brad, I might not have believed he would accomplish so much either! (Just kidding, Brad.) Unlike me, Brad had not been exposed to business from a young age—he was born into a family with absolutely no commercial experience. His father was a pastor, after all.

Brad was born in Sheridan, Wyoming, and moved to the Twin Cities when he was six. He attended a small Lutheran college in Iowa and, after two years, transferred to the University of Denver, where he studied sociology and history and earned his undergraduate degree. The following fall, at the urging of his father, Brad entered the Northwestern Lutheran Theological Seminary in St. Paul.

Brad soon decided that the seminary was not right for him; he dropped out after a year, in the spring of 1973. He says that he probably would have flunked out, but I doubt that. I believe he learned more there than he thinks he did. Although he knew he didn't want to enter the ministry, Brad was a classic 1960s kid who didn't want to follow a traditional career path. His wife, Janet, was something of a "flower child" who probably would have been happy living in Hawaii or some other beautiful place. But even though Brad and Janet were free spirits, they weren't exactly hippies and didn't really want to drop out of society like so many other '60s kids. So they decided to settle down in St. Paul.

Brad started looking for a job, something to tide him over until he decided what he *really* wanted to do with his life. He hoped to find a way to make a living that would enable him to continue learning and, above all, indulge his love of music. Brad was a music fanatic then, and he still is to this day. He listens to all genres and has encyclopedic knowledge of musicians and their work. On any given album, he can tell you all about the artist, when the tracks were recorded, and who the band members and sound technicians were.

Well, as fate would have it, Brad had purchased a stereo at our West St. Paul location, liked the atmosphere there, and decided it wouldn't be so bad to work in a music store. He applied for a job and was hired by the store manager, Herb Kyle, as a counter clerk and commissioned salesperson.

We didn't have a formal training program for clerks at the time, and there were only five employees at the store, so Brad was kind of thrown in at the deep end. I'm not sure if the manager knew that Brad had never sold anything in his life and had absolutely no retail experience. But if Herb didn't know, Brad soon made it abundantly clear. In his first two weeks on the job, he didn't make a single equipment sale on which he could earn commission, and he sold only a few inexpensive items at the counter. When he got his first paycheck, he couldn't believe his eyes—$69 for 120 hours of work, or about 57 cents an hour. (The wage laws have since changed, and no one could earn so little today. This is one of the reasons we eventually left behind the commission model—but we'll get to that story later.)

Brad was incensed. He couldn't believe that a college-educated person could be so bad at selling. Nor could he accept that anybody could earn so little money for two full weeks of work. It was frustrating for him and embarrassing, too. He went to the store manager and said he was going to quit. Herb told Brad to wait until they had a replacement for him.

I suppose Brad could have quit, but he didn't. Instead, he sucked

Brad Anderson in the early days.

it up and demonstrated the kind of perseverance that he would show again and again throughout the years. Here's how Brad tells the story:

> *"When I knew I had to stay for the next couple of weeks and I'd been totally defeated by this job, I thought, 'Well, what if I just did anything to make a sale?' That's when a customer came in and was going to buy a stereo, but he wanted it delivered and installed in Red Wing, Minnesota, which is substantially south of the Twin Cities. I would only make about fifteen dollars on the deal, but I agreed to deliver the stereo and install it for him. I had my first sale."*

That single transaction changed everything for Brad. He decided he was going to challenge himself even more. He got down to work, and pretty soon he was winning sales contests for us. After a few months on the job, he was promoted to assistant manager, and then he became manager. He stayed in that same store for more than seven years before joining us at headquarters.

Not only was Brad doing his job well, he was having fun—and so were his customers. Although we hadn't articulated our company values yet, Brad and his store certainly embodied one of the most important ones that we still live by today: having fun while being the best.

CRUISING ALONG

Throughout the 1970s, Sound of Music was a small, close-knit, family-style operation. In fact, the whole family actually *was* involved.

Sandy knew every employee by name. She was often in the stores, lending a hand, talking with employees about their concerns. We often had suppliers and staff members over to the house for dinner.

My father-in-law, Bob Larkin, who had invested in the company and was on the board, also played an important role in the company. Bob knew a lot about building and running a business. He was one of the officers of a company called Ecolab, originally known as Economics Laboratory, which deals in cleaning and sanitization products and services. (It's still going strong.) He was a cheerful guy, always chomping on a cigar, who loved to talk about business and the stock market.

In those days, I would try to get away from the office to play golf from time to time. It seemed that at every board meeting, Bob would start by saying, "Dick, I saw you on the golf course yesterday. If you're ever going to amount to anything, you better be in this damn office. You can't make money on the golf course!" Bob spent every Wednesday afternoon at the club. He'd be in the restaurant, and if he saw me heading out to the course, he'd yell out the window at me: "Get back to work!" After that happened a few times, I stopped playing golf (although I picked it up again later).

Our oldest child, Susan, who was born in 1965, started showing an interest in the business by the time she was four or five. She loved talking with Sandy about design and decor and would always come to new store openings. The two of them would sometimes bring their cleaning supplies to the office on the weekend so they could dust my desk and tidy up.

Starting in eighth grade, Susan started helping out in other ways. We had sales in the stores pretty often, usually on a Saturday, and we always needed extra hands. I'd call Susan and ask her if she could come with one of her girlfriends and look after the cash registers. She didn't mind at all and was a great worker.

Of course, there may have been other reasons that brought her in, beyond just helping out dear old Dad. I'll let her tell you:

> *"Back in those days—the late seventies, early eighties—it was all guys selling electronics. And a lot of those guys were really hot. They were out of high school, in college. And I was just getting into high school. So it was kind of interesting to meet these guys and learn more about the stores. Brad Anderson and part of his team actually came to my junior high school musical play, which was* West Side Story, *and filmed it."*

While Susan's initial interest in the business was all about boys, don't be fooled by that! She played a much bigger and more important role in the company later, and for many years.

In addition to the family members, many other great people joined us during the 1970s—and some of them are still with us. One of them was a young woman hired as a receptionist in the Bloomington office in 1979. Her name was Donna Mankowski, and yes, she's the same Donna who still supports me at the home office today.

Donna and I hit it off. She came from a farming family with ten kids. She was a hard worker and had the same values that I did. I had only a part-time secretary at the time, so I started asking Donna to do other things in addition to her responsibilities as receptionist. Everything I asked her to do, she did so efficiently and so well that I gave her more and more assignments. Not only did she complete everything expertly and on time, she also was frugal and understood the importance of keeping a close eye on costs.

That kind of performance was essential, because we didn't have any real systems in place then. Our inventory system, such as it was, involved calling each store every morning and recording the previous day's sales. Donna took over those calls. Then she got involved in making travel arrangements and negotiating with travel suppliers. Pretty soon Donna was involved in almost everything, from accounting to advertising.

By the end of the 1970s, Sound of Music, from the outside anyway, looked pretty healthy. We had grown to a staff of about fifty-five people, we were doing about $4 million in annual revenue, and we were operating in seven locations. I was making enough money to cover the mortgage and family expenses. I could even afford a Cadillac.

There was only one little problem: we were about to hit a rough patch.

HEADING FOR DISASTER

The problem was as much about the industry itself as it was about our company.

The consumer electronics industry was changing quickly in those days, with the move from records to cassette tapes, as was the whole nature of retailing in the United States. It was the beginning of the consumer age, when consumers were starting to demand better service, wider selection, and the lowest possible price—and were starting to get all those things. Wal-Mart was growing like wildfire, and the introduction of the "big box" era was not far away. In our industry, the small record shops and mom-and-pop electronics retailers were, one by one, going out of business, as chains like Circuit City and Highland were bringing all kinds of consumer electronics—from music to computers—under one roof.

So, as Sound of Music grew, we couldn't act like a little family business anymore. We were competing head-to-head with the two big players in the Twin Cities area—Schaak Electronics and Team Electronics—and they had some important advantages over us. They had deep roots in the community, so they knew the suppliers and the consumers very well. They also had deeper pockets than we did. As a result, both companies had much greater purchasing power with the suppliers than we did, which meant they could get volume discounts that we couldn't.

To match or beat our competitors' prices, we had to keep our cost of operations as low as possible. Schaak and Team stores were in the major malls and big shopping centers. Those locations were advantageous because of the heavy foot traffic, but they came at a high price in the form of mall association dues and a percentage of profits taken by the mall owners. So to keep our costs low, we generally stayed away from the major malls and sited our stores in strip malls and on commercial streets outside the major shopping districts. The result was that our sales, general, and administrative (SG&A) costs were much lower than those of our competitors, which meant we could match their sale prices and most often beat them.

We also had to learn how to deal with the cyclical nature of the consumer electronics industry. The cycles are the same today as they were then, although they're shorter now and everything moves faster.

A new technology is introduced at a high price point, and the early adopters, about 10 percent of the consumer population, line up to see and buy it. They're the ones who had to have the first Sony Walkman when it came out in 1979, the first big flat-screen TVs when they became available in the mid-1990s, the iPad as soon as it was available in 2010. The retailer makes higher gross margins on these hot new products.

If the technology catches on and everybody wants it, competitive products appear that are just as good or almost as good. The product soon moves to the discount channel, and the price falls quickly. It has happened to every type of electronics: audiocassette players, computers, VCRs, televisions, MP3 players, cell phones.

To deal successfully with the commoditization cycle you have to be smart about managing inventory.

First, you have to order the right merchandise, which means the products that the *consumer* really wants, not what the supplier really wants to sell you. This sounds pretty obvious, but the two things are often very different. Countless times a supplier would come to me and say, "Dick, I can offer you a great deal on this new product. If you buy a thousand units, I'll give you one whale of a good price." Well, a lot of retailers would jump on the bandwagon because the price looked so tempting. But I always asked myself what consumers would do with the product and whether they would really buy it. I never bought a new item just because a supplier wanted to give us a good deal.

Second, you have to order the right quantities. If you order too little, you're going to lose customers and leave a lot of money on the table, especially during the holiday season. If you order too much, you may never be able to move the products at full price, if at all.

Third, you have to place your orders at the right time. To be ready for the holiday, we had to start buying inventory in August or even earlier, or we might not be assured of getting what we wanted from the suppliers. But we wouldn't sell the merchandise until October, November, even as late as January, and the money could come in even later than that, if the consumers were buying on credit or we were offering extended payment terms.

In order to keep costs low, offer what consumers want, and manage inventory successfully, you need to constantly negotiate the best prices and most favorable payment terms from your suppliers. But many suppliers at that time specified in their contracts the exact price that had to be charged for any given product—the "list" price. If a competitor had negotiated a lower price, because of their higher volume, our hands were tied. Increasingly this became a problem for us.

"What if we cut prices below the list price?" I finally asked Elliot. "What's the worst that can happen?"

"They could terminate the relationship," he said. "They could stop selling products to us. They could sue us for breach of contract."

"What do we do then?"

"We could sue them for antitrust violations," he replied, "because I believe these suppliers are engaging in a form of price fixing."

So, from the mid-1970s on, we began setting our own prices, sometimes well below the manufacturer's suggested retail price. This put a strain on our relationships, to put it mildly. Sometimes they wouldn't give us the products we wanted in the quantities we wanted. Sometimes we couldn't get good payment terms. Sometimes they refused to extend credit. Some of them ripped up our contracts. Some of them sued us. And, as Elliot said we would, we filed counterclaims against the suppliers.

By the end of 1979, it all came to a head. We were almost out of cash. We owed a lot of money to our suppliers. Our cash flow just barely covered expenses. The banks were done with us. I had pushed everybody as hard as I could, and there was nowhere left to push. We talked about every possible option. Was there some other way to deal with the suppliers? Something else we could do to extend our credit?

Nobody wanted to say the word that everybody was thinking: bankruptcy.

THE FATEFUL MEETING AT THE DECATHLON CLUB

Finally I called a meeting.

It was Elliot and one of his partners, Howard Patrick, who specialized in bankruptcy, and me. We met at the Decathlon Club, a business conference center located in Bloomington, near our headquarters. We talked for several hours. Elliot and Howard said that we could file the papers very quickly, probably by the end of the week, and Sound of Music would immediately go into bankruptcy. We weren't talking about a reorganization or a temporary filing. This would be it. Over.

I didn't like it at all, of course, but it seemed like the only thing we could do. Elliot and Howard started preparing the papers on the spot. By 11:30 that evening, we were just about done. We were exhausted and unhappy. I just couldn't get my head around what was happening.

"Elliot," I said. "If we file these papers, we'll be stiffing some people, right?"

"Yes, you would be, Dick," he agreed. We would be walking away from our commitments, saying to our suppliers and creditors, *Tough luck. We can't pay. You're stuck with our bad debts.*

I didn't care how tricky our relationships were with our suppliers—that was something I really could not do. How could I hold up my head ever again? Who would want to do business with me? I have always thought of business as a competitive activity. To file bankruptcy would be a form of losing. I *really* don't like to lose.

I looked at the papers again. I made up my mind.

"I can't do it, Elliot," I said. "I just can't do it."

"What are you going to do?"

"I don't know yet."

Here's what I did: The next morning I got on a plane to Las Vegas, where the Consumer Electronics Show is always held. Over the next couple of days, I met with our key suppliers. I debated, discussed, negotiated. I managed to get some concessions. Then, once back in Minneapolis, I scraped together some personal funds and a family loan. All together, it was just enough to keep us going.

As I said, Best Buy was not always big, and we didn't always have a lot of cash. But we *always* kept our commitments. Somehow.

Although we got through that near-death scare in 1979, we hadn't really fixed the underlying issues. We were still strapped for cash, and we didn't have a clear view of what our future could be. We were just limping along, still essentially the same business we had been in 1966. The stores were still shoeboxes, selling primarily music-related merchandise. We had not yet learned about the absolutely essential importance of *transformation*.

Then, in 1981, nature helped us out in a curious and unexpected way. We got hit by a tornado.

It was the best thing that could have happened to us.

CHAPTER THREE

A TORNADO HITS—AND SO DOES A REALIZATION

I WISH I COULD SAY THAT I WAS A VISIONARY BUSINESS-person who always knew exactly what our customers wanted before they knew it themselves, but I wasn't. There aren't many visionaries like that in the world. Most of us have to achieve our success in other ways. In addition to passion, purpose, and perseverance, you just have to *listen to your customer* and try to respond when they tell you what is important to them.

The problem is that customers don't always know what they want until they see something new and fall in love with it. So you can be listening to them and responding to what they say and thinking you're satisfying them, when suddenly—*boom!*—everything changes.

That's what happened to Sound of Music in 1981. Since our founding in 1966, we thought we had done a good job of listening to our customers. Their wants were clear and didn't seem to change much over the years. We could satisfy customers if we delivered the products they asked for through smart negotiations with the suppliers and if we could sell at reasonable prices by keeping our costs low.

But as I've said, the whole retailing landscape was changing in the late 1970s and early 1980s, with the arrival of mass merchandising, big-box stores, everyday discounting, and the huge national retail chains. Although we saw those changes taking place around us, we didn't really know how they might affect us or our customers or how we might better compete.

It was on June 14, 1981, that we caught a glimpse of the future.

IT WAS THE WORST THING THAT COULD HAPPEN TO US . . .

It was a lazy Sunday afternoon on a typical early summer day. Sandy, the kids, and I had spent a nice weekend at our lake cottage, a couple of hours north of St. Paul, and were getting ready to drive home. I was listening to the radio when an emergency bulletin cut in: the National Weather Service announced a tornado watch for the Twin Cities area. The storm was headed for Edina, a town about ten miles southwest of Minneapolis where we had a Sound of Music store.

Minnesota doesn't get as many tornadoes as Texas and other states in "tornado alley" do, but they're not uncommon here. Still, I had never lived through one and didn't want to. I was concerned about our stores and especially about our people—employees and customers alike. Tornadoes can strike fast and be deadly.

I was worried. I told our family we had to leave immediately and get home right away. Susan, age sixteen, had a lot of friends around the lake. "Do we *really* have to go back now?" she moaned. But she helped Sandy round up the younger kids, and we all climbed into the van.

We listened to the radio the whole way home. Remember, there were no cell phones, no Internet connectivity in 1981. Our only source of information was the car radio. We listened as the tornado watch was upgraded to a warning, which meant it had already touched down at least once. Then we heard that the storm had reached Edina, where it had caused property damage . . . and then that it was headed north toward Roseville, where we had another Sound of Music store.

Just as we were approaching the city, the announcer came on again. A shopping center in Roseville had been hit hard. A restaurant had been severely damaged . . . cars had been turned upside down . . . *a Sound of Music store had been destroyed.* He went on to talk about emergency shelters and medical relief, but all I could think about was the store. What exactly had happened? Had anybody been hurt? What about the building? The inventory?

When we got home, the phone was ringing off the hook. I took calls from Brad and from Dave Telschow, the Roseville store manager. They both told me to get over there right away. I helped my family unload the van and then drove toward the Roseville shopping center. By then the tornado had passed, but it was still raining hard and there was evidence of the storm everywhere.

The police had cordoned off the whole area. "Sorry, sir, you can't go in there," an officer told me.

"That's my store," I said, pointing at the pile of rubble where the store had been. "I've got to check on my people."

"Your name?"

"Dick Schulze. I own the Sound of Music company."

"ID, please."

I showed the officer my driver's license.

"OK," the officer said.

I parked the car on the street and ran to the store. I couldn't believe my eyes. It looked like a bomb had gone off.

Brad was there, talking with Dave. Thankfully, nobody had been hurt. Dave told me that when the tornado hit, he had been at the counter waiting on a customer, a Russian gentleman who was interested in buying a stereo system. There were two salespeople in the

The Roseville store, after the 1981 tornado hit.

store and a couple of other customers. While Dave and the Russian customer were talking, without warning, the entire roof ripped right off. Speakers flew through the air and bounced off the walls like Ping-Pong balls. Everybody dove for cover. It was all over in a minute or two.

Dave knew that I was at the lake that weekend, so he had called Brad, who lived nearby. When the warning sirens went off, the whole Anderson family had hurried down to the basement, and they were still there when the phone rang. Brad had already gotten a call from our security company, saying that an alarm had been tripped at our Roseville store, so he wasn't surprised when Dave told him the news.

Dave showed me around the store. It was a disaster. Everything was upended. Boxes scattered everywhere. Speakers, television sets, turntables, and VCRs were thrown around. Power lines were down, and live electrical wires dangled dangerously throughout the store. Miraculously, the stereo counter and the car stereo area were completely intact.

We learned later that our store had been the final scene of destruction in the storm's path. According to public records, the tornado first touched down at 3:49 P.M. near the intersection of France Avenue and Fiftieth Street in Edina. A local policeman saw it hit and immediately called it in. The National Weather Service quickly issued the warning, and two hundred sirens began wailing in four counties around the Twin Cities.

The tornado roared northeast over Lake Harriet, headed straight for Roseville. Along the way, it generated winds of 80 to 160 miles per hour, which made it an F3 storm, or what they call "severe." The wind funnel bounced along—touching down hard, then lifting up again, then slamming down once more—snapping off tree limbs, tearing at power lines, and punching out windows as it went. After it hit the Roseville shopping center, the tornado approached a mobile home park, but just before it got there, it lifted off and, at 4:15 P.M., vanished. During those twenty-six minutes of wind and fury, many homes and businesses were damaged, eighty-three people were injured, and one young man was killed by a falling tree.

We later learned that the Sound of Music store in Roseville suffered the most damage of any building along the tornado's path. All we knew at the time was that we didn't have a roof, it was still raining, and all the inventory that hadn't been destroyed by the tornado would soon be ruined by water. We had to get the stuff out of there, fast. But there was no way that Brad, Dave, and I could clean it all up by ourselves. We needed help, big time. The phones were still working, so we started making calls.

About sixty-five people were employed by Sound of Music at that time, all of them in the Twin Cities area. Within a couple of hours, *sixty-three* of them showed up to help. They dropped what they were doing, grabbed whatever they thought would be useful, jumped in their cars, vans, and trucks, and drove through the rain and past the tornado damage, prepared to do whatever had to be done to aid our company.

We had one goal: get all the inventory out of the store as quickly as possible. How to do that? Load it into the pickups, stuff it in the backseats, pile it into the vans, and ferry it piece by piece over to the Sound of Music warehouse in Bloomington, about twenty miles away. We worked together, shoulder to shoulder: Brad, Dave, me, and—off and on, throughout the afternoon and into the evening— almost the entire staff of the company. At last, although the store still looked ruined, all the inventory had been removed.

The company may not have been in great financial shape at that time, but this experience proved we all cared about it a lot and were willing to pitch in to make sure it survived.

That meant a lot to me.

...AND IT WAS THE BEST THING THAT COULD HAPPEN TO US

Once we had gotten over the immediate problem of cleaning out the store, we had to figure out what to do next. Although our first concern had been for the people and the inventory, I knew that the damage could mean serious trouble for the company. The Roseville location, although one of our smaller stores in size, was second largest by sales volume. The building and its contents were covered, but we had no business interruption insurance, and so we would probably take a pretty big hit to our profits—perhaps as much as a 20 percent drop that year. That's significant.

I couldn't help but wonder, *Can we survive this?*

I had to keep telling myself that we would find a way to overcome this and rebuild our store's business. I had to keep in mind one thing: perseverance pays, for those who keep the faith.

It didn't take rocket science to figure out that we should have a sale on the distressed items. We could probably sell off the affected merchandise on an "as is" basis—at greatly reduced prices—and recover some percentage of our lost sales. So, over the next couple of days, our financial people worked closely with the insurance adjusters to work out a settlement. We found that a great deal of the merchandise had been so badly damaged that it had to be completely written off.

This did not bode well for our plan. There just wasn't enough saleable merchandise to make for a very impressive event. But wait a minute! We had lots of other products in the warehouse and in the stores. We had plenty of open-box items. We had many display items . . . discontinued models . . . overstock. What if we just grabbed everything, tornado-damaged or not, and marked it down?

It sounded like a plan. We decided that the best place to have the sale would be at the Roseville store location. We knew that people were fascinated by the tornado and had been driving into Roseville from all over, just to have a look around. What if we set up a big tent next to the store so we could let people have a peek at the ruined building? Remember: *listen to your customers!* If they wanted to see tornado damage, we'd show it to them.

We decided that we wouldn't try to make the sale look fancy. Instead, we stacked merchandise on wooden pallets in the parking lot and arranged most of the big stuff, like televisions, in a tent behind the store. We drove in a storage trailer, parked it out front, and loaded it up with turntables, speakers, and receivers. We lugged in cash registers from the other stores. We set up a string of portable toilets. The whole thing looked kind of like a county fair crossed with a funky yard sale.

And we advertised like crazy, on newspapers, radio, TV. *Tornado sale! Two days only! Get your BEST BUY on turntables, VCRs, speakers, tuners! Credit available!*

So, on June 20, the Saturday following that Sunday tornado, we kicked off the sale. As fate would have it, that morning there were tornado warnings all over the city.

We thought, *It can't happen to us again . . . can it?* It was raining off and on, and we ran around moving merchandise under the tent or covering it with plastic.

But it was just a scare. No tornado hit, and by midmorning, traffic was backed up for miles trying to get to us. People were driving in from all parts of the city, wanting to check out the blown-away building and hoping to score a great deal on electronic equipment. The parking lot was crammed with cars. The tent was packed with customers. At the trailer, a line snaked in one door and out the other. We had asked one of our business associates, Jerry Hable of

Customers loved the experience of the first tornado sale.

Suburban Credit, to set up shop in a trailer, and a queue of folks waited to apply for credit with him.

We worked our tails off all day long. Sandy was there, doing anything and everything. She helped people fill out their credit applications. When it rained, she broke out the umbrellas. When people got hungry, she appeared with stacks of pizzas. Susan was helping out, too. Her job was to collect cash from the cashiers and deliver it to our controller, Gail Ingram, who would count and record it. Susan loved clutching those big wads of bills.

I had never seen anything like it before, and I have never seen anything like it since. It was total madness. People didn't care what brand they bought. They hardly cared about the price. They just knew there was lots of stuff available, much more than they would normally find in our stores. They loved that everything was out in the open for them to look at, touch, pick up, and examine, rather than tucked away in the back room. They thought it was great that they didn't have to talk with any salespeople if they didn't want to or deal with the pressure to buy. There was an incredible amount of energy and excitement. There was even some friendly competition about who could grab what before the next person did. This was a whole different consumer electronics experience. It felt like entertainment, a place to be, a cool event.

Only one little problem: by the end of the day, we had sold almost everything. The stacks of VCRs and rows of TV sets and piles of speakers that had looked so attractive in the morning had now dwindled to almost nothing. And this was only Day One. What were we going to sell on Day Two?

I got on the horn to the warehouse. "We need more equipment!" I barked. "I'll be over later!"

As soon as we closed down for the evening, I drove straight to the warehouse. I walked through, pointing at equipment and boxes: "OK, let's take this one. And that one. Those over there, and that stack, too." By the next morning, when the doors reopened in Roseville (even though there weren't any doors left), we were restocked and ready to go. Let the madness continue!

When the two-day sale was over and we had a chance to catch our breath, the whole world looked different. We knew something pretty amazing had happened, but we weren't entirely sure what it was. We knew that we had moved a greater volume of merchandise than we ever had before—in fact, in those two weekend days we had sold significantly more stuff from that single location than we typically sold from *all* our locations combined. Wow!

Although we didn't fully understand it then, our customers were talking to us loud and clear. They were telling us that they had seen something different—and they *really* liked what they saw.

But what was it that really appealed to them? Was it the energy of the event? Was it the low prices? The open boxes? The big selection? The tent? The sales approach? All of the above?

Whatever it was, I wondered if we could recreate this kind of environment on an everyday basis. If so, maybe we could take our company to a place we had never dreamed of before. Maybe we could grow to $10 million in sales, $20 million, maybe $50 million! Maybe we could really knock the cover off the ball. Maybe we could blow the roof off the whole industry!

But how could we do that? Obviously, you don't get a helping hand from an F3 tornado every day. There had to be another way.

A MENTOR SHOWS ME THE FUTURE

With the memory of the tornado sale in my mind, and the dream of a whole new business model in my heart, Sound of Music struggled through the end of 1981 and into the new year.

We experimented with a bunch of things, and even ran a second big sale that we called Tornado Madness II, but everything we tried seemed like a short-term fix for a long-term business problem.

Brad took the academic approach, studying the changes in the retailing industry. In particular, he kept his eye on the national chains—Sears, Circuit City, Kmart, Sam's Club—as well as the regional competitors like Schaak and Team. One of the companies we paid close attention to was Highland, because it was growing fast, was based in the Midwest, and was operating with the "superstore" model. This referred to stores with footprints of 20,000 square feet or more, stores that offered a wide range of consumer merchandise—electronics and much more. Brad came to the conclusion that the specialty audio business, which is how we thought of Sound of Music, couldn't survive much longer.

I agreed with him. We needed a new strategy. We had to find a way to put into sustainable practice what we had learned from the tornado sale. We had to be ready for the competition from the big chains that was sure to come.

In search of new ideas, I decided to attend a weeklong seminar run by the North American Retail Dealers Association (NARDA) in Chicago in the summer of 1982. NARDA is a trade group made up of companies from various retailing businesses, including home goods, appliances, and consumer electronics. It's a not-for-profit organization that gathers and disseminates information, runs seminars, and generally supports and helps retail companies and their management.

At the NARDA conference, I was lucky enough to attend a session led by a gentleman named Ezra Landres, whom everybody knew as Zeke. A couple of years earlier, Zeke had sold his consumer electronics business, Certified TV, which was based in Norfolk, Virginia, to Circuit City, the chain that was getting a lot of attention

Zeke Landres.

at the time. Zeke joined Circuit City, known for its superstore format and aggressive expansion activity, after selling his business to them. But he wasn't impressed with the management of the company, so he left two years later.

Zeke loved retailing, though, so rather than retire and play golf, he joined NARDA and put his skills to work as a speaker, trainer, and consultant. His main focus was profitable retail management. He really understood the inner workings of the retail world, and especially the appliance and consumer electronics industry.

Zeke was a fantastic presenter, one of the best I've ever seen. At the seminar, he stepped up in front of the audience and let us have it, right between the eyes. No holding back—he called a spade a spade. He brought everything to the surface. He also had a dramatic physical presence: I guess he weighed more than three hundred pounds.

Zeke completely blew me away with his high energy and no-nonsense ideas. I went up to him at the end of the session and asked if he would be kind enough to come to Minneapolis and take a look at the Sound of Music operation. I'd show him what we were doing and how we were doing it, and maybe he could give us some thoughts about how we might change things so we could better compete, grow, and become more profitable. Well, I don't know if I had asked the right questions during the session, if he thought I was so naive that I desperately needed his help, or if he just took a liking to me, but he agreed.

Not long after the seminar, Zeke, good as his word, showed up in Minneapolis. I toured him around headquarters (which didn't take long) and walked him through the warehouse. We visited every store. He met a lot of our people. All the while, I found myself telling him how challenging everything was with us, how one-dimensional our business seemed to me, and how we needed to get out of our little boutique division of the industry and look at other ways of doing business.

Zeke listened patiently and looked carefully. Finally, he said, "Dick, it won't do any good to *talk* to you about what you could do better. I'll have to *show* you. I'm going to drag you to the East Coast and take you around some stores that will give you a sense of the future. That's the only way you'll get to the next level of opportunity."

What could I say? I was intrigued.

Not long after our conversation, I flew to Richmond, Virginia. Zeke and I visited Circuit City and Highland stores together, walked through some high-end specialty shops that specialized in TVs and appliances, and paid a visit to the chain that Zeke had built and sold to Circuit City.

As we toured, we talked. Zeke was big on the superstore concept. "Dick," he said, "Sound of Music needs to offer more kinds of merchandise. You certainly have to get deeper into television."

OK, that was pretty much a no-brainer. We already were selling some TVs.

"And you should sell small electrics, too. And appliances."

"Appliances?"

"Yes, appliances."

"But how does that fit with anything we're doing now?" I asked.

He ignored me. "You should also think about getting into computer software. I'm not wild about computers themselves, but software is good."

A lot of the stores we visited were selling cameras, which we hadn't touched at Sound of Music. "What do you think about photo equipment?" I asked Zeke.

"No margin in that business," he scoffed.

That's pretty much the way it went. Zeke and I spent several days together, and when we were all done, I was all fired up. I wanted us to have what the big companies had: the scale, the capital, the incredible buying power. And to get it, I was ready to expand our offerings and take those big players on, go head-to-head with them.

"Slow down, Dick," Zeke cautioned me. He understood the politics of the industry as well as he understood the nuts and bolts of products and retailing. "You're not ready to take on Circuit City and the other big guys," he said. "They're too big, too strong, too well connected. They'll crush you. They'll starve you. They'll force you out. Maybe later you can go after them, but for now you should fly under their radar. Build your business."

What I learned was that the biggest players were part of a consortium that gave them tremendous buying power. They would never let us in, and there was no way we could match their volume and clout. But as things turned out, we *did* take on the big players, and over the long run, we beat them—every one of them, one after the other. Those victories were particularly sweet because Zeke had warned me that we couldn't win against them. I guess I love proving to people that if something is right for our customers, I will find a way to make it happen. I will find a way to win.

I came away from that trip with Zeke wanting to learn more. The camera business in particular interested me, even though Zeke didn't think much of it. I had some friends on the West Coast who were in photo retailing, so I flew out there and visited several stores. I studied how they sold cameras and lenses and adapters and cases. I learned about the mechanics of the business and found out that Zeke was dead right: the margins were pretty low. Even so, I thought that photography—and eventually, digital imaging equipment—could fit well with our other offerings.

At the end of 1982, after this period of learning and reflecting, Brad and I sat down together. We knew that Sound of Music was at the very end of its rope. We said, "We need to get into all these new businesses. We need to do it all."

We figured we had one more shot at it, but we had to be bold. No baby steps. No incremental changes. No fiddling around. We needed a whole new approach—a larger store with a much wider selection and an exciting environment, and a company with much bigger ambitions.

We knew the concept had to be a winner. If it wasn't, we were finished.

A RIDICULOUS NAME FOR A COMPANY AND A TERRIBLE LOCATION FOR A STORE

First, we needed a great name.

The name Sound of Music had worked for us in the past, but now it was too limited, too narrowly focused on audio equipment and records and tapes. Plus, it was too associated with a small chain of specialty stores that had grown slowly and had never been terribly profitable.

What would be better? The phrase we had used during the tornado sale kept running through my mind: *Get your BEST BUY.*

I talked it over with Elliot. "We need a new name for the company," I said. "What do you think of Best Buy?"

"That's ridiculous," Elliot replied.

"Why?"

"Dick, how is anybody going to know what it refers to? Best Buy what? Best Buy clothes? Best Buy—what the hell are we selling?

Who's going to come if they don't know whether we're selling electronics or something else?"

I stuck to my guns. Why was I so sure about the name? Because getting a "best buy" on a product is very different from getting the lowest price—it implies value. I knew we couldn't necessarily beat the big chains on price, but I was sure we could always offer competitive prices and a great selection. What's more, the name gave us plenty of flexibility. We could sell audio, video, photo, computers, appliances, and whatever new kind of merchandise we wanted to sell in the future. So the fact that the name was not specific about our product offering was actually a positive thing.

"It's a good name, Elliot," I insisted.

By this time, he knew when it was no longer productive to keep arguing with me. "OK, Dick, it's your company," he said. "Call it whatever you want."

Next we needed a big building in a wide-open location. None of our Sound of Music stores was right. Even though we were in the process of expanding two of them, one in West St. Paul and one in Maplewood, they would still be small—10,000 square feet, tops. The chains were creating stores of 15,000 to 25,000 square feet. Besides, our stores didn't have sufficient parking capacity, and because they were in strip malls and on city streets, they weren't visible enough.

I looked around the Twin Cities area until I found what I thought was the perfect spot—a big, empty building high on a hill in Burnsville, Minnesota, just south of Bloomington, across the river. It was 50,000 square feet in total, 25,000 square feet of which were retail space. Best of all, it had fabulous visibility from Highway 13, which is a main east-west highway, and it was very near Interstate 35W, which runs north-south. Maybe the access wasn't so great, but it had a huge parking lot.

Elliot didn't like the Burnsville location any better than he liked the name Best Buy. "Where is it, exactly?" he asked.

"Just off Highway 13," I said.

"I'm going to drive out there right now and take a look."

When he came back, Elliot said, "Dick, that's a stupid location."

"Why? It's cheap!"

"Why? Because you can't get to it! You're driving down the freeway and you can't tell where you're supposed to get off. You drive right by the store!"

"The visibility is fantastic," I said. "Plus, with fifty thousand square feet, we can move the corporate office and the warehouse there."

"Dick, it's too damn far away from everything!" Elliot said. He was getting a little agitated.

"It's going to work great," I said with a smile. "Besides, it's done. We have a lease with an option to buy within eight months. It's a great deal."

Elliot likes to think that if he says something is the dumbest thing we could do, then I figure it has to be the smartest way to go. That's not really true, but I *was* right that time: the Burnsville store was a home run and incredibly profitable in its first year.

So we had a concept, a name, and an empty building. All we needed now was product and lots of it: cameras, appliances, software, home office equipment, computers (I ignored Zeke's advice on that one, too), televisions, VCRs—the whole enchilada. More kinds of merchandise, many different brands, and greater quantities than we had ever sold before.

Only one little problem: money.

Remember, we had almost gone under in 1979, and we had never really recovered. In fact, the recession years of 1980–1982 had been disastrous for us. We had literally burned through what profit we had made since 1966. And with many of our suppliers, we had run out of maneuvering room. In fact, we owed most of them money.

I went to every bank, every financing company, every private lender I could think of. Finally, I managed to secure a $100,000 line of credit from the Westinghouse Credit Corporation. I had to make a personal guarantee backed by virtually everything I owned. I didn't have to promise my firstborn, but pretty close.

The money wasn't much, but it was enough to secure a lease, with an option to purchase, on the Burnsville building, and to continue the expansion of the two Sound of Music stores. But $100,000 was nowhere near enough to buy all the inventory we would need to stock our first Best Buy store. For that, we would need help from the suppliers—not just the ones we already knew, but a bunch of new ones as well. They had to be willing to take a chance on the Best Buy concept, or it would never fly.

Why would suppliers risk it? For one thing, my history with many of them had fostered confidence. They trusted me. They knew I was as good as my word and always had been. They also knew that we had the passion, the perseverance, and the sense of purpose to make a go of almost everything we had tried.

But sometimes, in addition to convincing people with a dream, you have to have a backup plan in your pocket to influence the outcome. Once again, Elliot drew up bankruptcy papers. If the suppliers failed to come along with us into this new venture, we would simply go out of business. If that happened, the suppliers would have no way of recovering all of the money we already owed them. We figured they'd prefer taking a bit of a risk to suffering a certain loss.

In January 1983, I put the Best Buy business plan and the Sound of Music bankruptcy papers in my briefcase. I headed for the Consumer Electronics Show in Las Vegas, knowing that this would likely be our last chance.

CHAPTER FOUR

LAST CHANCE
IN VEGAS

L ET ME GIVE YOU A SENSE OF MY FRAME OF MIND AS I attended the Consumer Electronics Show in January 1983, because that episode taught me an important lesson: *leverage your strengths.*

What were our strengths in those difficult days?

Good question. It was much easier to see our weaknesses. Remember, as a company, Sound of Music was running on fumes. We had no working capital. Our cash flow was up one day and down the next. Our industry was changing rapidly, with new government regulations that were fueling the growth of national chains. As a result, our whole class of trade—specialty consumer electronics retailing—was going the way of the dinosaur. Over the next few years, almost every mom-and-pop shop and regional operator would disappear or be swallowed up by one of the big players.

But how did I feel personally? That's a whole different story. I was chock-full of energy and enthusiasm. I knew that our days as Sound of Music were numbered, but I truly believed in our new plan. After all, music was bigger than ever. That year, 1983, Michael Jackson's *Thriller* made it to thirty-seven weeks at the top of the charts, becoming the best-selling album of all time. (Nearly thirty years later, it still holds the record.) The computer category was growing fast, too, and so was gaming: Nintendo was already reporting billions of dollars in sales in 1983. I was convinced that a consumer electronics superstore, selling everything from stereo equipment to computers to dishwashers, all in a big, exciting retail environment—with everyday low prices—would be a winner. I thought we could become a $50 million company, maybe bigger.

And I refused to accept that the suppliers wouldn't go along with us. We had done business with many of them for ten or fifteen years. They respected our values and our ethics. They knew we kept our word and were reliable. They had always gotten paid—maybe a little late sometimes, but the check always showed up in the end. I wasn't going to turn my back on seventeen years of hard work, of serving customers, of building a reputation. If I had anything to say about it (which I did), we were not going to go out of business. *We would persevere!*

Brad had a different view. In fact, he thought I was crazy. Sound of Music was doing around $10 million a year at the time. Where would the $50 million come from?

"Brad," I said to him, "there's no question that this is going to work. We've done too many things too well, for too long, with too many great people. We will not fail. Look, if you deliver on what you say you're going to do—and you do it over and over and over again, as we have—people come to believe in you. So, when times aren't quite as good, they'll give you a shot."

Brad did not look convinced, but he said he would go with me to Las Vegas. Deep down, he thought Sound of Music was finished, but he had never been to the Consumer Electronics Show and he didn't want to miss it—especially as he figured it might be his last chance to attend!

So, three of us flew out to Las Vegas: Brad, Kurt Reedy, and I. Brad ran the retail stores, and Kurt handled marketing and merchandising. They were based at headquarters, and each of them also had managed a store—Kurt in Edina and Brad in West St. Paul.

As we flew across the Great Plains and over the Rocky Mountains, I kept thinking about our situation. In my briefcase, I had two folders, one for Plan A and one for Plan B. The Plan A folder contained a picture of the Burnsville location, a floor plan and merchandise layout, and other materials we had prepared. But it was pretty much smoke and mirrors. We didn't have a full-fledged business plan, with revenue projections and all of that. We simply didn't know how much business we could do.

In the Plan B folder was the bankruptcy filing that Elliot had insisted we prepare. "Dick," he had said, "you've got to have the bankruptcy option. It's the only way you'll walk away from seventeen years of hard work without losing your house. If you're wise, and I hope you will be, you'll put the filing on the table and show the suppliers it's ready to go."

I didn't like the idea of bankruptcy any more than I had in 1979, but I knew Elliot was right. The filing option was a negotiating tool. And if worse came to worst, it would keep me and my family from being thrown out on the street.

I knew it was going to be a tough three days, but I couldn't wait to get started. I was looking forward to the end of the show, too. Sandy was going to meet me at the Las Vegas airport so we could fly to California to spend a few days together.

Whatever happened at the Consumer Electronics Show, I guessed we would need some time off.

NEWS FLASH: SOUND OF MUSIC CLOSES ITS DOORS FOREVER?

Let me set the scene for you. It's a crazy one.

The Consumer Electronics Show—or CES, as everybody calls it—got started in New York in 1967 as a showplace for new products and technologies and a gathering spot for the movers and shakers in the industry. CES alternated between Chicago and Las Vegas from 1977 to 1995, when it moved to Las Vegas permanently. Today, it's the largest consumer electronics trade show in the world. Thousands of people from around the globe attend each year.

If you haven't been to this event, or one like it, it's almost impossible to imagine the scene. First and foremost, it's a massive trade show, a series of huge exhibition halls jam-packed with booths of all sizes. Everybody who is anybody in consumer electronics is there—retailers, manufacturers, service providers—showing off their latest products. Some of the booths are small, with just one person handing out business cards. Some of them are elaborate affairs with exhibition spaces, presentation areas, and meeting rooms.

And the biggest players pull out all the stops to attract your attention, with theatrical shows, multimedia programs, streaming videos, live music, magicians—you name it.

The CES organizers claim that thousands of new consumer products are revealed at the show each year. Many of the biggest breakthrough technologies have been unveiled there, including the VCR, the CD player, HDTV, Blu-ray, the tablet computer, and 3-D television. Off the exhibition floor, you can take advantage of an incredible array of educational offerings—dozens of big-name speakers, forums and seminars, and expert sessions on every imaginable topic.

Being at the show is both electrifying and exhausting. It's like a county fair, superstore, sales convention, lecture hall, and Broadway show all rolled into one. Add to that the casinos, nightclubs, and stage extravaganzas of the Las Vegas surroundings, and you begin to understand why CES is the go-to event for the industry.

But at that show in 1983, I wasn't particularly interested in looking at the new products. I didn't care about the seminars. I had no intention of poking around in booth after booth. My mind was

A scene from the 1983 Consumer Electronics Show.

focused on one thing and one thing only: convincing our creditors to support our new venture.

In addition to everything else, CES is also a meeting place. People are constantly doing deals, networking, negotiating contracts, building relationships, and sometimes having disputes and cutting their ties with one another. They meet on the main floor, in the private meeting spaces, in hotel conference rooms, and in the restaurants and bars. It's all deals, deals, deals—constant deals being done.

And that's what I was there for. I needed to meet with at least a dozen companies that sold many different kinds of merchandise, from audio gear to computers. We already did business with some of these companies, and unfortunately, we owed most of them money. Not a lot—no more than $100,000 to any one of them—but still, we were in their debt. I also needed to try to establish relationships with certain companies. I had managed to make a number of appointments in advance. But with some of the suppliers, I would just have to show up . . . and wing it.

We arrived at the show early that first morning. The plan was for Brad and Kurt to work the floor, check out the booths, talk with suppliers, place orders for interesting new stuff, and generally act like everything was OK with Sound of Music. Meanwhile, I'd be working behind the scenes, hammering out the arrangements one by one.

Well, you know what they say about the best-laid plans . . .

Our cover was blown almost immediately. We got to the exhibition hall and picked up a copy of the *CES Daily*, the newspaper that covers the show. On the front page, in the lower corner, we saw a headline that almost made my heart stop. It read: *Sound of Music Closes Its Doors Forever.*

What? Where in blazes did that come from? We hadn't talked to any reporters. We hadn't told anybody we were going out of business. Could the story have been a plant? Was somebody spreading rumors about us? Why? If the suppliers believed we were going out of business, how would that affect my negotiations?

I was livid—and I don't know, maybe that gave me extra energy. I told Brad and Kurt I'd see them later, and off I went to give it my best shot.

WHICH DO YOU CHOOSE: PLAN A OR PLAN B?

I won't tell you about every meeting I had during the first two days of the show. I can't remember them all, but each one went pretty much the same way.

I'd locate the booth of the company I wanted to meet with. The major suppliers' booths were easy to find, because they stood out above the rest. They were usually laid out in a big square, with

merchandise displayed around the perimeter and a two-story structure at the center, where the offices were located. I'd introduce myself
and be taken up a set of stairs and ushered into a meeting room. It
was usually small, nondescript, and claustrophobic.

In would come the company rep. Sometimes it was the national
sales manager, sometimes the president or CEO, but most often it
was the credit manager. If we didn't know each other, I'd introduce
myself and we'd chat for a couple of minutes about the show and
then about the business in general. Then I'd get down to my plan.

Here's an example of how things went at one meeting.

"Look," I said, "Sound of Music has been in operation since 1966—
almost seventeen years. In that time, we've built the company up to an
annual revenue of about ten million. We've done business with your
company for a long time. We've always kept our promises, always paid
our bills. We really value our relationship with you. Maybe we're not
the most formidable company in the consumer electronics business,
but we're an important player in the Twin Cities market."

Pause. So far, so good. Now the hard part.

"But," I continued, "everybody knows the consumer electronics
business is changing fast. The technology cycles have gotten shorter.
Our small company is now competing with superstores and national
chains. We have been stretched to the point that we have no liquid
capital left. Our equity is literally gone. All the earnings we retained
over the past few years—gone. We're up against the wall."

Gulp. No liquidity? No capital? That is not something suppliers
like to hear, especially when you owe them money. I could see the
credit manager thinking: *Maybe that article in the* CES Daily *was
accurate. Is this guy Schulze going to tell me he can't pay? Is he here
to announce that Sound of Music is, in fact, going bankrupt?* I could
feel the tension building in the room.

"OK. That's the bad news," I said. "Now, here's the good news:

we've put together a really exciting plan for a whole new business model. Our stores are small now. The biggest one is about eight thousand square feet. Our new one will be three times as big—twenty-five thousand square feet of retail space. A *superstore*."

I pulled out the Plan A folder and showed him the floor plan.

"Right now, we focus on stereo and TV. In the new store, we're going to offer a much broader assortment of products. We're going to get into imaging, video, and VCRs. We'll offer cameras and camcorders and a wide variety of other merchandise. Consumer electronics will still be our main focus, but we're going to expand way beyond those products."

The credit manager muttered, "Mm-hmm."

I kept going. "Right now, our main customer is the young male, eighteen to twenty-five years old. In the new business, we're going to be selling to a much wider audience, with a concentration on the female consumers who are largely responsible for more than fifty percent of all goods and services purchased in the United States. Right now, we're selling at competitive prices. In the new store, we're going to offer deep discounts, just like we did at our tornado sale two years ago. People went crazy. We moved more merchandise in one weekend in one location than all the other stores combined."

At this point, the credit manager was listening, but his head wasn't nodding.

"Look, everything's in place, ready to go," I said. "We've negotiated a lease for a great building in a high-visibility location." I showed him a picture of the Burnsville building, high on the hill. I didn't mention the problem with access, or that Elliot thought it was a stupid place for a store.

"We have a new name," I went on. "I'm confident this can work."

A long silence.

Finally, the credit manager looked at me as if I were completely nuts and said, "Dick, I thought you said you have no capital. How

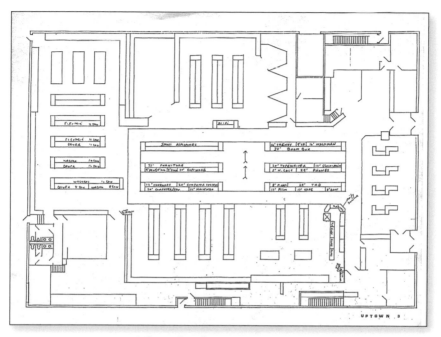

A floor plan for a Best Buy store.

are you going to pay for all this? Especially when you already owe us money."

Fair question. Obvious question. The question I had been expecting.

"Well," I replied, "I have a line of credit with Westinghouse Credit Corporation."

"How much?"

"A hundred thousand dollars."

"A hundred thousand? Secured by what?"

"My personal guarantee."

"Your personal guarantee? Your house?"

"Yes."

"That's a start, but a hundred thousand is not enough for what you say you want to do. Where are you going to get the rest?"

Pause. Now we had arrived at the moment of truth. "Well," I said, "that's where you come in."

"That's where *we* come in? What do you mean? We?"

Nothing to do but say it flat out: "I want you to extend our credit terms. I want you to ship us the product we need in our new store. We'll sell as much of it as we can, as fast as we can. We'll use the cash flow to pay our expenses first, then to buy more product from other suppliers, and then to pay you. It may take eighteen months, or it could take twenty-four months, but I give you my word—you'll get paid in the end."

Now the credit manager looked at me as if—in addition to being totally nuts—I had also been smoking something. He took a deep breath. "OK, Dick, let me get this straight. You mean to tell me that you want us to give you time on future purchases when you haven't even paid what you owe us today. Is that right?"

"Yes. That's right."

"And you're going to take the proceeds from the sales of *our* product and you're going to pay somebody else for *their* product?"

"Yeah, that pretty well summarizes it."

Long silence. The credit manager cleared his throat. He looked down at the table. Shook his head. "Well, Dick, I have to say, this isn't feeling real good."

"Well," I said, "if I were in your shoes, I guess I'd say the same thing."

"Mm-hmm."

"But you have to understand. This is the only way for us to be able to field a stronger assortment, create bigger stores, sell to a more diversified customer group, and have a chance at surviving the challenges of the day."

"Mm-hmm."

"I know this requires a leap of faith on your part. But I need you to recognize that we've built up a lot of trust over the years. Not just with you but with all of our suppliers. We have a long history and a lot of experience. This is a major initiative to leverage who we are. It's an opportunity to start fresh. I know it sounds crazy, but we'll pay you what we owe."

"Well," the credit manager said at last. "Let me take it under advisement. Let me talk about it with my people. We'll let you know."

"OK," I said. "Thanks very much for your time."

"Sure." The credit manager got ready to leave.

I decided it was time to play the card that Elliot had prepared for me. "One more thing I need to tell you," I said.

"OK."

"You should know there is an alternative to this plan."

"What's that?"

I opened my briefcase and pulled out the Plan B folder.

"Bankruptcy," I said.

"Bankruptcy?"

"That's right." I showed him the filing papers. "If you don't extend our credit, we'll have no choice but to file at the end of the week."

I let the credit manager look over the papers. He could see that this was not a filing for a reorganization of the company. It was a liquidation. If that happened, their company would get, at best, pennies on the dollar—and at worst, nothing. What's more, the word would get out: *Did you hear that XYZ supplier wouldn't give Schulze what he asked for? They wouldn't extend his credit. They pulled the cord on him. He had no choice but to go out of business. Nice guys to do business with!*

"So," I said, "either you're going to have to trust us, or we're going to have to file for bankruptcy. If you trust us, I won't promise exactly when you'll get paid, but I promise that you will. Everything we owe you now, plus everything we *will* owe you on the basis of future purchases."

I guess I had gotten his attention.

"OK, Dick," the credit manager said. "I'll get back to you. I'll let you know."

"That's all I can ask. Thanks very much for listening."

"Oh, and you said you're changing the name of the company?"

"Yes. We're going to call it Best Buy."

"Best Buy?"

"That's right."

We shook hands. Then it was on to the next booth and the next credit manager and the next presentation.

MEANWHILE, BACK ON THE FLOOR . . .

While I was running from meeting to meeting, Brad and Kurt were spending time on the floor—but they weren't having much fun. They were going from booth to booth, looking for merchandise we could feature in our stores in the coming year. But it seemed that every-body had read the article in the *CES Daily*. When they realized that Brad and Kurt were from Sound of Music, suppliers avoided them like the plague.

At one point, as I was cooling my heels, waiting to see a credit manager, I saw Brad wander into the same booth, although he didn't see me. He started checking out the products, on the lookout for the next gee-whiz breakthrough, the next must-have offering for our stores. Of course, all the time he was thinking, *Can we actually buy anything? Will anybody sell to us? If they do, can we pay for it?*

While I was watching, a company rep came up to Brad, said hello, and started discussing the products. After a minute or two, the rep glanced at Brad's badge. I could see the guy's face fall and could almost read his thoughts: *Sound of Music? Didn't I read that com-pany is going out of business? Closing all its stores?* After about two minutes, the rep excused himself and left Brad staring at the equipment. After another minute, Brad quietly slipped out of the booth.

It was a tough three days for all three of us. As the show went on, more and more rumors spread. People saw me hustling in and out of meetings. They watched Brad and Kurt trying to act cool. Everybody guessed that something was up, but they didn't know what. Maybe they liked us personally, but they just didn't know what to say or how to deal with us. By the second day, when people saw Brad coming, they would literally turn and walk in the opposite direction. It was not good for his ego. He and Kurt toughed it out, but they couldn't accomplish anything worthwhile, and it was very frustrating for them.

Meanwhile, I was so busy that I didn't have time to update them on my progress. During the first two days, I met with twelve credit managers. At some point on the second day, I don't know exactly when, credit managers from most of the largest vendors met as a group to talk over what I had proposed. I wasn't invited, but I heard about it later. They asked one another, "What do you think about Sound of Music? What about Schulze? What about this deal? What do you think?"

After a fair amount of discussion, they came to a conclusion. "Well, we like the guy. He's done great work for seventeen years. The company has never defaulted on any of its promises. They pay their bills. Yes, they've had their issues. No, we don't like what he's proposing. But the alternative is worse. He showed us the bankruptcy papers. He's obviously not bluffing."

A couple of the credit managers didn't agree at first. But ten of the twelve fell in line, and finally the other two weren't willing to put the kibosh on the deal. By the end of the show, although we hadn't finalized the details and didn't have signed contracts, we had the commitments we needed.

On the third day of the show, I finally connected with Kurt and Brad. I was exhausted. We went to dinner together, and I told them the news. The suppliers had agreed. We had a window of about eighteen months. We'd get terms we could live with. The suppliers would ship the most critical goods we needed. We had a chance.

My colleagues were both delighted and skeptical. Brad knew this was the only way the company could survive. He was thrilled we were going to have a shot at turning things around. But Brad was also curious. He couldn't quite believe that the suppliers had come around. So, after the show, he asked a number of them why they had agreed to the deal. I'll let Brad tell you what they said:

> *"The suppliers said that, at the end of the day, it was Dick. It was all about Dick. The plan didn't really make total sense to them. And in truth, the plan probably wasn't a world-beater, because we didn't have enough of it together and we didn't have any real evidence it was going to work. I personally thought all the evidence was against it. So, it was purely a bet on the individual, the human being, that the suppliers were making. They bet on how much he believed he was going to make it happen.*
>
> *I discovered a lot about Dick at that show. Here's a guy running a very unhealthy company, talking about the fifty-million-dollar company we were going to build. I couldn't see the seed of a fifty-million-dollar company, let alone the five-billion-dollar or the fifty-billion-dollar company that we became. But Dick had this enormous sense of confidence and vision. He was a driven, confident entrepreneur. And the Las Vegas show was the turning point, a huge turning point. If that hadn't happened, there wouldn't have been a company."*

I've included Brad's flattering comments about me for a reason: before you can leverage your strengths, you have to understand what they are. Going into the Las Vegas show, I knew that we were weak on finances and organization and on a formal business plan. But I also knew we were strong on vision, commitment, and talented, hard-working people. And as it turned out, those things carried the day.

BULLET DODGED

Of course, we still had a lot of negotiating to do. The suppliers wanted security guarantees and payment schedules, and we needed to finalize the purchase terms and credit limits. The suppliers wanted to tie us up as tightly as they could. We wanted as much room to maneuver as we could get.

But all that could wait for a couple of days. I drove to the airport to meet Sandy, who was flying in from Minneapolis. She knew all about what had been going on, how worried I was, and how close to bankruptcy we were, but she didn't know yet that I had been successful in the negotiations. Even so, she came off that airplane smiling as though there was no other place on earth she'd rather be than Las Vegas, and as though Sound of Music was in the greatest position it had ever been in. We went on to California, and she never let on to anyone that there had ever been an issue. In her mind, there was nothing we couldn't overcome, wouldn't overcome, and couldn't always overcome.

After that show, I thanked my lucky stars. I thanked Elliot for insisting that we prepare the legal papers. I thanked Brad and Kurt for suffering through three days of hell. And I thanked Sandy for being such an incredible supporter.

Talk about leveraging your strengths! When it came down to the wire, all we had was our values, our reputation, our vision, our relationships, and the great people on the Sound of Music team. But that was enough—more than enough.

Now, of course, we had just eighteen months to make good on our promises. I really hoped that Elliot was wrong about that store on the hill.

CHAPTER FIVE

BEST BUY
IS BORN

YOU MAY HAVE NOTICED THAT I BEGAN EACH OF THE first three chapters of this book with a disclaimer: *I wish I could say that I was a visionary businessperson . . . I would like to be able to say that I began Best Buy with a unique vision and a brilliant business plan . . .* Well, I would like to start this chapter by saying that our big new Best Buy store, located at the top of that hill in Burnsville, was an immediate success when it opened in 1983—and the nice thing is, I *can* say that. The store *was* a huge success, right from the start.

I *can't* say, however, that we knew exactly what we were doing all the time, because (as Brad will soon attest) we didn't. Nor can I say there were no hiccups, because there were plenty of them. But it's hard to argue with the numbers. In its first year, that single store achieved $14 million in revenue—$3 million more than the entire chain of Sound of Music stores had taken in the year before. We were trucking!

For the first time in our seventeen-year history, we had really hit the cover off the ball. It was an incredible feeling. And although we couldn't imagine it then, the success of that single store marked the beginning of a remarkable run of revenue and profit growth for Best Buy, and the launch of our "big box" era. Today the Burnsville store remains a mainstay for us, on that very location, nearly thirty years later.

At the time, Elliot thought the idea was nuts. Now he tends to agree with me that the stars were aligned for us.

OPENING DAY MADNESS

We set the date for the opening of the Burnsville store for Saturday, October 1, 1983. That meant we had about eight months after the Consumer Electronics Show to get everything ready. And there was a lot to do.

We had to develop relationships with many new suppliers, including photo equipment manufacturers like Minolta, Nikon, and Canon; appliance companies including GE, Whirlpool, and Maytag; and computer makers IBM and HP. We also had to negotiate terms, make deals, and place orders with all our current suppliers. Plus, we were thinking about all kinds of additional categories—cookware, watches, quartz heaters, video rental, home office products, and who knows what else.

We also, of course, had to fit out the store itself. And we really were not clear on how to do this. Should we display the merchandise by brand? By price point? By profitability? Should we organize the televisions by screen size or by furniture style? (Those were the days of the console TV, when the screen was set into a fancy wood cabinet.) As for displaying stoves and video cameras and computers, we had virtually zero experience.

We certainly didn't understand the flow of customer traffic in a space so large. The Sound of Music stores were simple: You walked in the door and everything was right there, in an area about the size of your average Starbucks today. To fit out a store, all we had to do was spec out the shelves, figure out where to put the sales counter, install carpet, and do the lighting and electrical work—and that was pretty much it. The service department, if you can call it a "department," was typically in the basement, out of sight. Inventory was kept at the warehouse. Once we had the basic template down, setting up a new location wasn't rocket science.

Burnsville was different. Not only would the store be ten times larger and have many additional categories of merchandise, but we wanted to create a totally different kind of selling experience. The Sound of Music stores were pretty intimate; the feeling was somewhere between a college dormitory room and a young couple's living room, complete with music playing in the background. We wanted the Best Buy store to be bright and fun, lively and open. We wanted to capture the crazy feeling of the tornado sale, combine it with the hustle and bustle of the Las Vegas trade show, and also give our customers a sense of the incredible assortment and value of a superstore.

That's where Pat Matre came in.

Pat was our facilities manager at the time (he's still with Best Buy, as our VP of real estate) and had been working with the company since 1979. Pat came to Sound of Music the way a lot of employees did back then: pretty much by chance. Pat was brought up in Chicago and attended Loyola University there, studying English and philosophy. After graduation, he traded in his degree for a hammer, as many children of the 1960s did. He found work as an independent contractor, building out restaurant locations for the Old Spaghetti Factory chain. After ten years of roaming the country for Old Spaghetti, Pat and his wife settled in Minneapolis, which was her hometown. In addition to his Old Spaghetti Factory jobs, Pat started picking up residential work—building decks and home additions.

In 1979, before Best Buy was born, we needed to do some remodeling at our West Lake Street store, a single-story box near downtown Minneapolis. At the time, Sound of Music didn't have a facilities department or a full-time facilities manager. My brother, Bob Schulze, was building our display units for us (as he still does), and when we needed to install the units or get any other kind of building work done, we hired an independent contractor. One of the salespeople at the West Lake Street store suggested we hire Pat Matre, who was a friend of his. Pat came in and installed new shag carpeting (it was the '70s, OK?), set up display units, hung shelves, and did whatever else needed to be done. He did a fine job and became our go-to contractor for other work throughout the chain.

We soon discovered that Pat also knew a lot about audio equipment and about music in general, so when we weren't keeping him busy with building and remodeling, he would fill in as a part-time salesman. He managed the West Lake Street store for a time while continuing to work as an independent contractor.

Eventually, it became clear that we had enough work to hire a dedicated facilities person. Besides, I thought we could control our costs better by bringing Pat on board as a full-time employee. I asked him to come in and have a conversation about it. Here's how Pat remembers that interview:

> *"I was probably billing Dick about fifty thousand dollars' worth of work a year at that time. But I had my expenses, like my truck, so I wasn't clearing very much. Dick was a pretty tough negotiator.*
>
> *Dick brought me into his office, with its dark wood paneling and shag carpeting. He said, 'Pat, what would you need to hang up your tool belt and come work for us on salary?'*
>
> *I said, 'Twenty thousand dollars.' That was a pretty decent salary in those days. He said, 'How about twenty-five thousand?' I guess that was the only time in Dick's life when he negotiated* up."

Why would I offer Pat more than he asked for? Because I knew that he was a special person and that he would contribute a great deal to our success over the years, which he has. Our success at Best Buy has always been the result of the good people who have become part of our team. In Pat's case, he has become a legend in the world of retail real estate. (I hasten to add that I don't offer too many people more money than they ask for. I wouldn't want that to get around. It would be very bad for my reputation.)

So, in 1983, when it came time to build out the Burnsville store, the responsibility largely fell on Pat's shoulders. Looking back, he says that he thought what we were trying to do was "incomprehensible." But he dove right in. We brought in the goods, created new fixtures, carpeted everything, built the displays, put in electrical connections, and installed new lighting in the ceilings. We arranged the traffic flow so people walked by the warehouse and the service department as they entered the store. We wanted them to see that we had lots of inventory and that we were well prepared to service the goods we sold. We displayed the merchandise on open shelves—rather than behind counters—so customers could take time looking over and evaluating our products.

We weren't sure how many of the categories that we put in place would actually pan out. We thought the photo products and entertainment software might set us apart from our competitors, but we couldn't know with any certainty at the beginning. When we were done with the build-out, we were excited. We felt that we had created a wonderful world of entertainment for this fantastic range of new Best Buy products.

At last, the big day arrived. We opened our doors that Saturday morning, and it was a madhouse all day long. What I remember vividly was the parking problem. Even with that big parking lot, which had looked so huge to me when I first saw it, we didn't have enough

We always make a big deal out of a store opening.

spaces for all the cars. People drove in from all over. When the lot filled up, they parked their vehicles anywhere and everywhere they could find a spot—on the access roads, on the ramp from the highway, along the boulevard that ran by the store, on the grass at the edge of the lot. It didn't take long for the city police to get word of this. They showed up and started writing tickets as fast as they could. A bonanza for the city coffers! Of course, the customers got very ticked off when they left the store and found a ticket under their windshield wiper. They'd hustle right back in and complain. We responded by offering them gift certificates (there was no such thing as a gift card at the time), which made them a little bit less irritated with the situation. What else could we do?

As amazing as the opening event was, I'm sorry to say that Brad had no more fun that day than he did at the Consumer Electronics Show in Vegas. Seems that one of the first people through the door that morning was Ron Graham, head of the Better Business Bureau for the Twin Cities. He suspected that Best Buy was going to engage in shady practices, and he was there to keep an eye on us. The first Best Buy person he saw was Brad, so Ron latched onto him.

I have to admit that there was good reason for the Better Business Bureau to be suspicious. Our building had a dubious history. It had been built by a company called Kennedy & Cohen, an electronics retailer that was trying to establish itself in the Twin Cities market. Kennedy & Cohen had engaged in various kinds of questionable practices. One of the company favorites was bait-and-switch advertising. To attract customers to the store, Kennedy & Cohen would advertise a very low price on an item; then, once the customer arrived, the salespeople would say the item was no longer in stock. Then they'd pressure the customer to buy a more expensive product. Ron got on the company's case, and after two years, it went out of business.

But it wasn't just that one consumer electronics company that was engaging in questionable retail practices. The whole consumer electronics industry—in fact, much of consumer retailing—was known to pull a fast one on the consumer from time to time. Retailers would bait and switch, or advertise a discount to a fictitious manufacturer's list price, or offer a super deal on a not-so-hot model that no one would ever want to buy otherwise. So I can't blame the Better Business Bureau for assuming that Best Buy could be up to no good.

Brad was no doubt the very best guy to deal with the issue. Here's how he remembers opening day in Burnsville:

"Ron Graham of the Better Business Bureau was completely convinced that we were crooks—mostly because we were so ill-prepared for what we were doing. He could walk around the store and find all sorts of holes in the operations—like not having enough inventory. These holes could have been

indications we were actually crooked, or they could have been signs that we were just inept, which is what we actually were. Although it took a long time to convince Ron we weren't crooked, we eventually became friends."

I can guarantee that Brad is right—any mistakes we made were ones of *omission*, not commission. We were definitely onto something, but we surely did not have our act completely together on that first day.

NEW LOOK, TRADITIONAL PRACTICES

Now, although our first Best Buy superstore *looked* a whole lot different from the Sound of Music stores, our operating approach hadn't changed as much as it might have appeared. In one important way, that was a good thing: we continued to run a very low-cost operation.

I had been a zealot about cost control from the day we opened the first Sound of Music store. I didn't change when we became Best Buy, and I'm still that way today. I'm sure I got the trait from my dad. Like him, I never wanted costs to get away from us. And as the commoditization cycle shortened, cost control became even more important. When you keep your costs down, you have a much lower threshold to meet each month. You also have a lot more wiggle room when it comes to purchasing and pricing.

By staying out of the malls, keeping our staffs lean, and creating much of the advertising ourselves, we had been able to seriously reduce our sales, general, and administrative (SG&A) costs—which includes everything from rent to payroll to advertising and marketing. SG&A costs are important because they are the dollars that are under a company's control—unlike the cost of goods, which a company can negotiate but does not ultimately control. Over the years, we had gotten our SG&A down to below 12 percent of revenue. That number may not mean much to some readers, but people in any retail business know this is impressively low. At the time, our direct competitors were running an SG&A as high as 28 percent.

In addition to running a low-cost operation, another thing that didn't change when we became Best Buy was our fundamental approach to sales. Although the Burnsville store was much bigger and more open, and it had more kinds of merchandise for sale than the Sound of Music stores did, we still followed the traditional retailing model.

That meant two main things: warehoused inventory and commissioned salespeople. In our Best Buy stores today, the bulk of our inventory is displayed on the sales floor, and the customer can grab a box and take it to checkout. They may never interact with a salesperson if they don't need to or don't want to. At the Burnsville store in 1983, however, we had one of each product model on display and the boxes were piled up on the warehouse shelves. As was typical of the time, the salespeople were paid a base salary draw against a percentage of each product sold—usually between 3 percent and 5 percent. This was the model that all the big consumer electronics stores followed, including the two big ones, Circuit City and Highland.

Taken together, these two aspects of the sales model had a big and sometimes problematic effect on how salespeople worked and how customers were served. The salesperson would almost always try to steer the customer toward the product that paid the highest commission. What's more, because the product was kept at the warehouse, the customer had to wait while the salesperson arranged for the item to be brought to the store.

Much of the time, the system worked well. Although a good salesperson might start by recommending a high-commission product, he or she would ultimately sell the customers whatever they wanted. But the system also made it possible for an overly aggressive salesperson to direct a sale. Have you ever heard of a spiff? A spiff (also known as a "spiv") is an incentive that a manufacturer offers a salesperson for selling a specific item. Company A, for example, might pay a $10 incentive for every VCR (*videocassette recorder*—the predecessor to the digital video recorder of today) the salesperson sells during a certain period of time. Company B might be offering a smaller incentive, or none at all, during the same period. If it's a popular product and the salesperson can move a lot of them during the day, the commissions can add up fast.

No question that a spiff puts temptation in the salesperson's way. He or she might push Company A's product a little harder than usual—or might even be tempted go a little further. For example, sometimes the salesperson would make an arrangement with the guys in the warehouse. When a customer asked to buy a Company B VCR, the salesperson would pick up the phone and call his buddy.

"Say, can you send me over a Company B VCR in such-and-such a model?" the salesperson would ask.

The warehouse person would look out the window and say, "Gee, I don't see any of that particular model right now." Of course, if he turned around and looked at the shelves, he'd see a hundred of them.

"Oh, well, how about the Company *A* model so-and-so?" the salesman would continue.

The warehouse guy would look back at the shelves. "Oh, yeah, we've got plenty of those. I can send one right over."

Done. The customer is happy enough. The salesman gets the spiff. If you look up the word in the dictionary, you'll see that the spiff has been around since the middle of the nineteenth century. A tailor would pay a spiff to one of his assistants for moving outdated or discontinued cloth. So don't blame the consumer electronics industry for inventing this practice! Obviously, I never condoned it, and we got rid of the practice at Best Buy.

The traditional retail model, despite its faults, worked just fine for our first few years as Best Buy—from 1983 to 1988. In fact, it worked much more than fine. The Burnsville store was like a house afire. The company rocketed. Oh man! It was one of the most exciting times in my career.

Not that we were totally out of the woods. It took us about eighteen months to pay off our creditors, but we finally did it. Even so, we still didn't have a lot of working capital. And it took us some time to figure out the right product categories and best assortment. For three years, the VCR was the hottest product in the store, bigger even than color television had been when it first came out. Millions of VCRs were being sold throughout the country, and plenty of consumer electronics chains were expanding on the back of VCR sales. We figured that because VCRs were so hot, video rental would also be a strong business for us. We were wrong. Video rental did do well, but mostly in small local shops, not in a superstore located high on a hill with inconvenient access.

Still, our sales took off. In our final year as Sound of Music, we had total revenues of about $10 million. In fiscal year 1984, our first with the Best Buy store, we took in $28,508,000. We turned a *profit* of more than $1 million!

When things are moving that fast, everything changes. I knew we had a huge opportunity in front of us. I also knew we needed help to take advantage of it.

BUILDING A TEAM

Now we were a $28 million company, run by two guys who really didn't have the background needed to run a company this large. You could say that I got my business training as a manufacturer's

My business card, circa 1984.

representative and a paperboy. Brad had a degree in sociology and had dropped out of the seminary. Those employees who weren't working in the stores were squashed into small offices in the Burnsville building, which were a little bigger than your average closet (but not much). We had a *very* shallow management bench.

We began by beefing up our board of directors. At the time, the board consisted of me; Elliot; Joe Francis; John Schwarz, an independent financial consultant; Bob Larkin, Sandy's dad; and Zeke Landres. Zeke had joined the board in 1983, not long after our trip together to explore the emergence of big-box consumer electronics stores. I started looking for another director who could bring strong management experience to the board.

One of our bankers suggested that I talk with a fellow named Frank Trestman. He was chairman and CEO of Mass Merchandisers Inc., a publicly traded company doing about $80 million in annual revenue. He also had served on the boards of several public companies—in distribution, finance, technology, and medical products—and had sat on not-for-profit boards. I met with Frank and told him about our plans. He knew little about Sound of Music and had just begun to hear about Best Buy. He thought our plan was doable, although he knew we had plenty of competition. Frank joined the Best Buy board in 1984 and served superbly for twenty-six years until he retired in 2010—helping us immeasurably in growing from $28 million to $50 billion.

In addition to building the board, Zeke was constantly on my case about strengthening our management team. Sure, Brad and I had done OK in managing Sound of Music. But Brad was primarily responsible for sales and marketing, and I was focused on the big picture—expanding the company. We had neither the time nor the skills to manage the financials of such a fast-growing operation. Our finance department consisted of exactly one person, a controller named Gail Ingram, who had been with us for many years and had pretty much grown up with the company. We didn't have any systems or controls to speak of. Very little was computerized. The salesman who made a sale was also the one who rang it up at the cash register. In other words, we were running our new rocket ship as if it were still the Dinkytown Sound of Music store. We needed someone who really knew finance and understood business operations.

To find the right person, we did what you did in those days when you were looking to make a hire: we placed an ad in the newspaper. We were lucky enough to get a response from a fellow named Allen Lenzmeier. He was working as vice president of finance for Perkins Restaurants at the time. He had started with Perkins in Minneapolis, and when they were acquired by Holiday Inn, Al had moved with them to Memphis. After about a year, he had decided he wasn't comfortable with the city or the company, and began looking for a new position.

Brad and I liked Al's resume, but I had one immediate concern: How much was it going to cost to fly him in from Memphis for an interview? Fortunately, I had a connection at Perkins. Bob Fox, who had been with the financial firm that audited Sound of Music, had worked with Al when Perkins Restaurants was in Minneapolis. I called Bob and asked if I should shell out the money for the plane ticket.

Bob said, "Dick, don't worry. It will be the best investment you'll ever make."

We bit the bullet and flew Al in. We met a quiet, self-assured, experienced guy of about forty. He had grown up in Minneapolis and had attended Mankato State University. Like Brad, he had attended seminary and then taken a different path after graduating. He had started his career at Price Waterhouse, the big audit firm, and then moved on to the National Car Rental System. He decided he didn't like working for such large companies and left to join Tom Thumb Food Markets, a chain of supermarkets, drug stores, gourmet food shops, and convenience stores that was just starting to get hot in those days. Al wore many different hats for the company, including setting up a computerized inventory control system and overseeing security and personnel. After six years with Tom Thumb, Al joined Perkins Restaurants, where he was employed for six years.

We showed Al around the company and took him to that year's Tornado Madness event. I don't think he had interviewed anywhere else. He joined Best Buy in the fall of 1984. Here's how Al remembers his first few months with us:

"During the interview process, Dick showed me his five-year plan. He told me he was going to get to $500 million in five years. But in the first six months I was with Best Buy, we were so far off plan that I kept thinking, 'I don't know what this guy is doing, but he must be doing the wrong thing, because he's way out of his mind in terms of where he thinks this business is going.'

But then things started clicking. We converted more of the Sound of Music stores to Best Buy. Our revenues began to increase. We actually started meeting those goals. And we hit that $500 million within the five years—easily. We started

*at about $25 million, and then we doubled, and then we basi-
cally doubled every year."*

REAL MONEY

With Frank as a director and Al as VP of finance and operations, we
had significantly strengthened our management team. But in order
to achieve our goals, we needed something more. We needed what
we had always needed and had never been able to generate: *capital.*
We wanted to convert all the Sound of Music stores to the Best Buy
brand, open new and bigger locations, and expand geographically—
throughout Minnesota, then to other areas in the Midwest, and
then . . . who knows?

Our revenue was soaring, but our expenses were climbing, too.
And we also continued to pay off our Sound of Music debts. I knew we
couldn't accumulate enough capital from profit and cash flow to catch
the expansion opportunity. There was only one thing to do: go public.
Yes, technically we were already a public corporation with shares available locally over the counter. But we hadn't done another stock offering
since that first one in 1969. Sound of Music shares weren't listed on
any stock exchange, and besides, they weren't worth a whole lot.

So, as soon as Al came on board, we got started on our first
public stock offering. After selecting the firm of Dain Bosworth as
our banker and doing the technical work, Brad, Al, and I set off on
our first road show. We told our story to all the major brokers in
Boston and New York. None of us had ever done a public offering.
None of us had ever participated in a road show like this. We didn't
know the players. We didn't completely understand the process. But
we had two things going for us: First, we completely believed in our
plan, and we were totally committed to making it happen. Second,
the market for our products was taking off.

As part of their due diligence, the brokerage houses sent research analysts to Minneapolis to check us out. These analysts could see the synergy that our array of products created on the floor. They could feel the tremendous energy in the Burnsville store. What's more, it was obvious that we had a huge opportunity in the Midwest. There was nothing like Best Buy in Iowa, Wisconsin, the Dakotas, Nebraska, Kansas, or Missouri. Sure, there were other large-format specialty companies like ours—Circuit City, Highland, and many others— but they were doing business in urban areas outside the heart of the Midwest: Detroit, Chicago, Indianapolis, Dallas, Houston, Atlanta, Richmond, New York, Los Angeles. Wall Street loved the different opportunity we represented: *Best Buy is going to do in the Midwest what we know has worked in other areas.* The brokers also might have liked our product assortment and our differentiation, especially with music and movie software. But mostly they saw a big, honking opportunity—an open pathway through the Midwest.

I loved making our pitch, fielding tough questions, and convincing the East Coast brokers that this little Midwestern company could be the next big thing. We thought it was going well, but we were still a bit shocked when we managed to complete the offering in April 1985. When the dust settled, we had sold 650,000 shares at $13.22 a share, bringing the company a total of around $8 million. We were ecstatic. Finally, we had some working capital. At long last, we had some leverage. After nineteen years, we were no longer living on cash flow. No longer did we have to take from Peter to pay Paul.

Going public was also a meaningful event for me personally, because it was the first time in almost two decades of doing business that I personally took any money out of the company. My salary had inched upwards over the years, and I was making around $50,000 in 1985, which was pretty good. I had deliberately plowed all our profits (when we had them) back into the business. But now I felt I could take

some money out. I was forty-four years old. Sandy and I had four children. We had been living in the same house in West St. Paul since just
after we got married. College tuitions were not too far away.

I owned about 75 percent of the stock, so I sold $1.8 million
worth of my shares, which reduced my ownership in the company
quite significantly. I put $1 million into a trust fund for the kids. And
Sandy and I bought a new house in Edina for $599,000 cash, where
we lived for the next eighteen years. Before the stock offering, Sandy
had said, "Dick, we shouldn't buy that house. It's too expensive. We
don't have the money." She was very conservative in that way.

I said, "Don't worry, we'll have the money. We'll pay cash. No
loans." And that's exactly what we did. I have to admit that it felt
really good.

ON FIRE

From that opening day at Burnsville in 1983, Best Buy grew like
crazy. We soon discovered that, along with the capital and excitement that came along with being a publicly traded company, there
were also lots of new responsibilities and requirements. One of them
was the annual report. At the end of each fiscal year (which, for us,
began in April) the company had to produce a report describing its
operations and presenting its financial results.

We issued our first Best Buy annual report in April 1984. (It
has that camera lens logo on the cover.) When you look through the
reports sequentially, starting in 1984, you see a pretty amazing progression of financial growth. We marched from $28.5 million in sales
in 1984 to $56.1 million in 1985 to $113 million in 1986. How often
is a company able to *double* its sales for several years in a row? Our
profits climbed to just over $4 million in 1986. And as we opened
new superstores outside the metro area, our average revenue per

store also climbed. In 1984, we did about $3.4 million per store. By 1986, the average was at $10.6 million, three times as much.

Everything about the company grew. By the end of 1986, we had grown from hundreds of employees to more than a thousand. We stocked 1,750 different products from 150 manufacturers—up from just a handful of product lines back in the Sound of Music days. We were into microwaves and freezers, dishwashers and clothes dryers, cameras and printers, along with our TV and audio gear. We were investing nearly $2 million in computer systems to better manage our inventory and distribution. Our stock was doing well. Our income per share climbed from 10 cents in 1984 to $1 in 1986, a tenfold increase.

The superstore concept was working, without question. In a photograph in the 1986 annual report, the three of us—Brad, Al, and I—look confident and satisfied with our company's success.

Of course, you can't achieve that kind of growth and success without a lot of people contributing and taking notice: employees, investors, shareholders, customers, the press. It seemed that all the attention was positive.

But not everybody was pleased with the growth of Best Buy. When we were a small, slow-growing, single-city operation, the other players in the consumer electronics business didn't pay much attention to us. But as we began to take off, we blipped on the radar of the big regional and national chains. The very companies we had been modeling ourselves after—particularly Circuit City and Highland—took notice of this upstart that was growing so fast.

Soon enough we learned that getting too much attention is not always a good thing.

CHAPTER SIX

SHOWDOWN

W E BEGAN HEARING OMINOUS RUMORS IN THE WINTER of 1986: *Highland is coming to town.*

Highland Superstores Inc., that is. The biggest and oldest and (supposedly) toughest consumer electronics company in the Midwest. Based in Detroit, Highland had stores concentrated in what we Midwesterners thought of as the "East"—Michigan, Ohio, Indiana, and Illinois—as well as Texas. The company had never shown any interest in the Twin Cities before. Why would Highland want to open stores in Minneapolis now? There could be only one reason: they wanted to squeeze us out before we grew too big. We were a threat. We were growing too fast. We had to be stopped.

This was an entirely new experience for us. We had always had competition, especially from Team Electronics and from Schaak. But we *knew* those companies and their management. They were local. The competition among us was certainly real, but the stakes weren't so high. The game was intense, but fair.

Highland was different. They were the big boys, and we were the little guys. At the time, Highland operated some fifty-three stores and had about $656 million in annual revenue. It was the second-largest national consumer electronics chain, after Circuit City, and had been growing fast. After it went public in 1985, Highland had a pretty substantial war chest. By contrast, we had twenty-four stores and sales of $169 million. We had low costs, but we carried a fair amount of debt.

Highland made the rumors official in March. They announced they would open three superstores in Minneapolis in May 1987. They would also establish themselves in Milwaukee, just three hundred miles away, at the same time. They were coming after us, no doubt about it.

We knew that Highland would follow the strategy that big retailers always use to destroy smaller ones: They would site their stores directly across the street from ours. They would offer essentially the same merchandise as we did. They would make a lot of noise through their advertising. They would undercut our prices. Highland might not make a nickel of profit, but they wouldn't care. Their game would be to steal Best Buy customers, build market share, monopolize the suppliers, and slowly suffocate us. Or maybe not so slowly: in a year—two years, tops—Best Buy would be history. Highland would declare victory.

Or so they thought.

I had a gut feeling that this was going to be the fight of our lives. We had a little over a year to get ready.

BRAD CHECKS IN TO MOTEL 6

The first thing we had to do was get smart about Highland. One of the most important lessons I've learned over the years is this: *know your competition.* Know who they are, what they're doing, what they're not doing. What their strengths and weaknesses are. How they think. How they behave. What their values are.

The best way to know your competitor is to dive into the belly of the beast. Don't guess what they're doing. Don't assume you know how they operate. You have to go to where they live. You have to observe them. Interact with them. Get to know them. Go through their trash, if it comes to that.

I knew there was only one man for the job: Brad.

Brad always seemed to land the plum assignments! He was the guy who hung out at the Consumer Electronics Show, getting the cold shoulder from suppliers. He was the one who took the heat from the Better Business Bureau on opening day at Burnsville.

Now he bravely, eagerly, took on the Highland assignment. He would go to Chicago, because Highland had a number of stores there. He would stay until he'd learned everything there was to know about the enemy. He would study Highland's merchandise . . . its store lay-outs . . . its salespeople . . . its management structure . . . its advertising . . . its promotions. How it sold. How it switched customers to more profitable products. *Everything.*

Of course, we already knew quite a bit of the basics about Highland Superstores Inc. The company was founded in 1933 by Harry Mondry in the Highland Park section of Detroit. It was called Highland Appliance in those days, and sold a range of household appliances at discount prices. After World War II, Highland expanded into consumer electronics and other kinds of merchandise.

In the early 1980s, the company experienced a growth spurt, thanks to a new product called the "microwave oven," introduced by Litton Industries. Everybody in America seemed desperate to have one. Highland got another boost, as we all did, from sales of the VCR. After Highland went public in 1985 (the same year we raised $8 million to expand Best Buy), the company got very ambitious and started to expand fast. It marched into New England and faraway Texas and got interested in the Midwest, too.

In 1986, when it decided to come after us, Highland was managed by descendants of the founder. Harry's son, Eugene Mondry, was chief executive officer. Gene's brother, David, was chairman. Gene's son, Mitchell, was in charge of customer service, and David's son, Ira, was chief operating officer. It was quite the family operation.

I will say straight out that Brad and I were not big fans of the Mondrys. Brad had met Gene in 1981 when Panasonic invited a number of retailers to San Francisco for a few days of education and entertainment. Brad was all excited because it was his first junket. At one of the dinners, Brad was seated across the table from Gene Mondry.

"Who are you?" Mondry asked Brad. He was known for his imperious tone.

"Brad Anderson," Brad replied.

"Who do you work for?"

"Sound of Music," Brad told him.

"Sound of Music? What's that?" Mondry didn't look very interested. He obviously had never heard of us.

"We're a small specialty audio chain," Brad said.

"Where are you located?"

"Minneapolis."

Mondry looked slightly surprised. "No kidding. Minneapolis? I like Minneapolis. That's a wonderful market. You're lucky to be there. That's just the kind of market we like to be in."

After that San Francisco trip, Brad bumped into Gene two or three more times. Gene would always do his best to put Brad down. He would call him "son." He would make a point of saying how much he liked Minneapolis. He would imply that someday Highland might deign to enter our market.

So Brad was, in his words, "massively motivated" to get the goods on Highland. In the spring of 1986, he checked into a Motel 6 in Chicago and spent the next month studying every aspect of Highland's operations. He posed as a customer. He purchased products from every category. He studied the company's ads. He did cross-shops, which meant comparing Highland's prices to those of its competitors.

He applied for a job and went through an interview. He bought service plans and extended warranties. He talked to salespeople, managers, service technicians, and customers. And he *did* go through the trash, looking for sales slips and pricing bulletins and internal memos and daily sales reports. All totally legal activities. All very revealing results.

During that month, I'd call Brad daily. "Brad, what are you doing? What's going on? I haven't heard from you in days!"

"I know. I'm almost done," he'd say. "I've only got eight more stores to go." He refused to come home until he had visited every Highland location in Chicago.

When at last Brad got back to Minneapolis, the man was a walking, talking encyclopedia of Highland Superstores information. He knew everything about what the company sold, where and who it came from, how Highland sold it. He could tell you, chapter and verse, what Highland did *with* the customer, *to* the customer, and *for* the customer.

There is absolutely no substitute for that kind of direct knowledge. I still visit competitors' stores regularly. (I visit our own stores, too.) I check out the merchandise. Study the prices. Observe the salespeople. Get a sense of the environment. Chat with customers. It's the best way, by far, to understand what your competitors are up to. You can never learn enough.

I implore everybody at Best Buy and every other company: *know your competitors*. Learn their strengths and weaknesses. That knowledge in itself is a competitive advantage.

THE ST. VALENTINE'S DAY MASSACRE

During that same period, we got a dramatic look at what going out of business looked like. In the spring of 1986, Schaak Electronics, which had been operating in the Twin Cities since 1960, closed its doors forever.

It's a sad story, really. I knew the Schaak family well. I was in high school at the same time as Dick Schaak, who became president of the company after his father's death. My dad had worked with Lee Schaak, Dick's father. I had clerked in one of the Schaak stores in 1959 before I went to Colorado to finish my training in the Air National Guard.

Schaak had a good business going, but the company made a fatal mistake. Remember the commoditization cycle I've talked about? Well, that's what brought Schaak down. Around 1980, Dick Schaak had gotten very excited about the future of personal computers. He told me that he wanted Schaak Electronics to become the biggest personal computer retailer that also sold consumer electronics. The company opened several stand-alone computer locations under the name Computer Den. Those didn't work out, but Schaak continued to build its computer inventories in its regular stores. By 1983, Schaak had computers in more than fifty locations throughout the Midwest. Riding on the back of its relationship with IBM, then the leading computer manufacturer, Schaak went gangbusters in 1984.

But then everything fell apart. Lots of other retailers were getting into computer sales, including some of the big chain stores. Many other manufacturers were offering products similar to those of IBM. Schaak Electronics had a lot of money invested in its computer operations and inventory and could no longer get the high gross margins it needed. In the spring of 1985, Schaak's share price wobbled. Dick Schaak tried to get out of the business. But this was followed by management battles, banking struggles, and problems with vendor relationships. At last, Schaak filed for bankruptcy and closed many of its stores.

It all came to a head on Valentine's Day—February 14, 1986— just around the time we were hearing the rumors that Highland was coming to town. Schaak Electronics abruptly closed its remaining twenty-one stores and let go 250 employees. We purchased the company's entire inventory: forty-eight truckloads of merchandise, everything from computers to boom boxes.

On Friday, April 25, 1986, we held an enormous sale at the Minneapolis State Fairgrounds in St. Paul. It was an unbelievable event. An article in the *Minneapolis Star Tribune* wrote that customers "turned out in such numbers that Snelling Avenue leading to the fairgrounds turned into a parking lot and Interstate 94 was snarled, the State Patrol said. At the normally deserted fairgrounds, buyers were lined up seven abreast and four blocks deep . . ."

The Schaak liquidation was even more amazing than our first Sound of Music tornado sale had been. We took in about $1 million in sales in that single day, about twice what we had expected. That was good for us financially, of course. But the sale was also a warning. I knew the Mondrys of Highland would be more than willing to hold just such a liquidation sale for Best Buy someday.

I should say that Schaak Electronics was hardly the only consumer electronics company that declared bankruptcy or was liquidated in the 1980s. Computer Depot, Pacific Stereo, Silo, Federated Group, Tech Hi-Fi, and Crazy Eddie all went down. They succumbed, in different ways, to the difficulties of running a high-volume retail operation: high-priced goods, large inventories, the

The consumer electronics industry experienced a big shake-up in the 1980s.

138 / BECOMING THE BEST

commoditization cycle, debt held by banks and creditors, lots of competition, and shifting consumer demand. By my count (which, I admit, has not been verified!), *576 consumer electronics retail businesses* went out of operation in one way or another between 1983 and 2000.

Today, in the United States, Best Buy is the only national consumer electronics chain left standing.

THE MOVE TO MILWAUKEE ... BY WAY OF NEW YORK

We knew we couldn't just sit on our hands and wait for Highland to ride into town and take us down. Brad had gathered a lot of information. Now we had to take action.

The first thing we had to do was to get all our Twin Cities stores ready for the fight. That meant enlarging the three that were still of "conventional" size (less than 10,000 square feet of selling space) into superstores of 25,000 to 40,000 square feet. That would take a couple of million dollars—money we didn't have.

Second, we had to cut our expenses to the bone. We already had a low SG&A of around 17 percent. One of the reasons for this was that we typically chose locations where we did not have to pay mall fees or sales percentages to our landlords. But when we expanded as Best Buy, we had taken on three locations that required payment of 1.5 percent of gross sales to the property owner. We were stuck with those payments, but everything else we would have to trim until we could trim no more.

The third step was bolder. We already had plans for expansion into the states surrounding Minnesota: North and South Dakota, Nebraska, Iowa, Missouri, and Wisconsin. Well, what if we moved into Wisconsin first? And what if, instead of starting with stores in Eau Claire and La Crosse, the cities closest to us in Minneapolis, we hopped straight into Milwaukee? Furthermore, and here was the bold part, what if we opened our stores in Milwaukee *before* Highland opened its stores there? Highland had announced a May 1987 opening. Why couldn't we be up and running by the holiday season of 1986?

And beyond Milwaukee, what if we accelerated our expansion plans? What if we pushed hard to open superstores in Des Moines and Davenport, in Moline and St. Louis? What if we built our volume and our customer base? Wouldn't that send a message—*Best Buy is not going to play defense*—to Highland or anybody else?

It sounded good, but we needed more money to do it all. A *lot* more. So, in May 1986, we went out with our second stock offering in two years. This time we thought even bigger than before. Working with Kidder Peabody, we issued a prospectus offering 1,375,000 shares at a price of $26.25 per share. After fees and other costs, that would bring in about $33 million. With the money, we would convert the three smaller Twin Cities locations to superstores. And we could commit to opening as many as twenty-four new stores in five states outside Minnesota over the next two years. Along the way, we would hire about six hundred new people to add to our existing force of 1,750 employees.

This time we listed on the New York Stock Exchange. Sandy and I traveled to New York with Brad, Al, and Elliott and their spouses, as well as other members of the Best Buy team. We met with Dick Grasso, then-chairman of the Exchange. And in due course, I got handed one of those huge cardboard checks printed with the amount $33,600,000. We had a fabulous celebration dinner at the end of the day.

Now we had the money, but we didn't have much time. I called on Pat Matre to take on the assignment.

"Pat," I said, "we need some real estate in Milwaukee."

"I'm on it, Dick," Pat replied, always up for a challenge.

"Highland is going to open three stores there in May. I want to open our stores by the holidays."

"By the holidays? You mean, by Christmas?"

"I mean the day after Thanksgiving. Black Friday."

Pat looked at me blankly.

"So," I said, "let's go to Milwaukee and find some properties."

"OK," Pat said. "I'll get that organized."

"I mean right now."

On the Fourth of July weekend, Pat and I climbed aboard a chartered aircraft along with Gary Holmes, a real estate developer we often worked with, and flew from Minneapolis to Milwaukee, a distance of about three hundred miles. We met a local real estate agent at the airport. We hopped in his car and drove around the city, looking for locations. We were assisted in our quest by the hottest new thing in consumer electronics: the cell phone. These gadgets were as big and heavy as small bricks, but they came in handy. We'd see a FOR LEASE or FOR SALE sign, pull up, take a look, and call the broker listed on the sign.

We knew roughly what we were looking for. Pat had gotten advice from one of his associates in Milwaukee: "You need three stores to cover the entire Milwaukee market. One in the west, one in the north, one in the south. The store in the west will do really well. North will be marginal. South will do fine. You don't need east, because that's Lake Michigan."

By the end of the trip, we had identified three properties. One was a plot of open land near the Northridge Mall. The second was a three-story motel, located on the west side of Milwaukee, across from Mayfair Mall. The third was a former AT&T switching facility on the south side, right across from the Southridge Mall.

It took until Labor Day to close the deal on all three properties. We immediately plunged into construction on the Northridge site. It was the most straightforward, because the land was open and we

I try my hand at construction.

could build from scratch. The other two sites were more complicated. We had to demolish the existing buildings. At the Southridge
site, we had to remove tons of telephone equipment. For both, we
had to secure all kinds of construction permits from the city. By the
time we got everything organized, there were exactly *twenty-eight*
days left to build our Southridge store from the ground up.

In order to meet our deadline, we realized it would be wise to
give the masons a little incentive to keep the work moving along. We
decided, however, that money would not be the most powerful moti-
vator. Instead, we bought a bunch of tickets to Green Bay Packers
home games and awarded them to the workers at the end of each
week, as they met one construction target after another.

Pat and his team performed like champs. Feeling the pressure of the Highland threat, they worked nonstop, flat out. Their commitment was an inspiration to me and to the rest of the company: *Look what we can do when we set our minds to it!* It had taken ten months to get the Burnsville store ready. Now we could open a store in less than *two* months. With the Milwaukee experience as a model, we could expand incredibly quickly. If we could do twenty-four stores in two years, as we had planned, how many could we do in five years? Ten years? Twenty years?

We opened three stores in Milwaukee on the day after Thanksgiving 1986, six months before Highland opened its doors in that city. People lined up around the block to get in.

So far, so good.

THE BATTLE BEGINS

Highland was not subtle about its attack on us. In early May 1986, amid much advertising fanfare, Highland Superstores opened its Twin Cities locations. The newspapers were full of the story: "Ladies, Gentlemen: Highland vs. Best Buy" read a headline in the *Star Tribune.* Gene Mondry was quoted in the article, sounding as haughty as ever:

> *"We think the economy is pretty strong in the Twin Cities, and demographics are good for a company like ours . . . If we look over the competitive situation, other than Dayton's and Target and a few others, the competition is Best Buy. They're a fine company, but we think we have things to offer. We offer in-home service and have our own service department. We are a much larger company and have access to lower prices than Best Buy, and we can pass on those savings to customers."*

He might as well have called the reporter "son."

All three Highland locations seemed to have been chosen to spit in the face of Best Buy. One store was on South Robert Street in West St. Paul, near the store we had been operating there since 1966. The second was in Minnetonka, nor far from ours. The third was in Brooklyn Center, just north of Minneapolis and, you guessed it, shoulder to shoulder with Best Buy.

Just as we expected, Highland's stores followed the classic model the company had been perfecting for decades. Nicely carpeted stores. Showroom atmosphere. Bait-and-switch advertising. Helpful salespeople directing the customer to the product with the most profit and the highest commission. The approach had worked for them in the past. Why shouldn't it work now? Why shouldn't it work forever?

The one deviation from the classic model was the super-low prices in these Highland stores, lower than in its other locations in other cities. When we saw them, it was hard to believe that we could hold out for very long. We estimated that Highland was pricing almost everything we sold at just 10 percent above cost. That was in comparison to the typical superstore markup of between 25 percent and 30 percent over cost.

Highland was obviously showing off its clout with suppliers. The company was part of NATAM, a buying consortium of the four largest consumer electronics firms in the world. (We weren't a big enough player at that time to play at that level. Instead, we were a member of Nationwide Television and Appliance Associates Inc., a buying group of smaller retailers with less power.) And Highland could also sell at such low prices because it could leverage its stores outside our markets and were willing to make little or no profit on their Twin Cities operation for as long as it took to finish us off. We could come close to these stores on price, thanks to our low costs, but there was no way we could match them, item for item. We didn't even try.

But price isn't everything. OK, it's *almost* everything when it comes to consumer electronics, but there are some other things customers care about. They want assortment. They expect service. They respond to a good shopping experience. They expect four things: low price, convenient location, assortment, and high-quality customer service. They want to trust the people they deal with. And, as we learned, they want to root for the hometown team.

This is where the Best Buy people in the stores played a heroic role. Sure, Brad and I and the others at headquarters orchestrated the strategy, but the real battle was fought on the floor of the stores, seven days, six nights a week. (Closed on Sunday evening!) Best Buy people poured their hearts and souls into their jobs. If they had to do double duty to keep costs down, they did. If we couldn't afford stock handlers in the stores, the salespeople would meet the trucks, offload the merchandise, and load up the shelves themselves.

One of the heroes of the battle was a young man named Brian Dunn. (You may recognize the name. He became our chief executive officer in 2009.) During the time of the fiercest competition with Highland, Brian was assistant manager in the Minnetonka Best Buy. He had joined us in 1985, primarily because his mother, Ethel, had badgered him into it. She worked at Best Buy in the co-op advertising department and loved the company. When Brian graduated from high school in 1984, his mother suggested he apply for a job with us.

"There's a lot of cool stuff going on at Best Buy," she said. "It's a very interesting place, and I know you could do real well there."

It took him a year, but Brian finally took his mother's advice. He was hired as a commissioned salesperson in the Minnetonka store. He sold televisions, VCRs, and "fully featured" remote-control units. (They actually had just two control features: power on/off and channel up/down.) After fifteen months on the job, Brian was promoted to team leader and then to assistant store manager.

So Brian was in the thick of things when Highland came to town. Every day, Brian would walk over to the Highland store, which was right across the street, to check their prices. We had cracked the code of their commission structure. All you had to do was reverse the product number displayed on the sign, and it revealed the price where commission kicked in. Every day, the manager of the Highland store returned the favor with us by doing exactly the same thing. We all knew him. He was a good-looking fellow and, like the Mondrys, he seemed to think highly of himself. The Best Buy employees called him Big News. He'd march toward the Best Buy store to do his due diligence, and everybody would whisper: *Here comes Big News again!*

It was a spirited period for Best Buy. Although the threat was real, it was also a fun and tremendously energizing time. I knew, however, that we couldn't rely on high spirits and esprit de corps forever. We needed to find something else to differentiate ourselves—some other way to really change the game. I just didn't know what it was.

A REVELATION

One afternoon in the late 1980s, as the Highland battle was raging, I had an experience that sparked a whole new way of thinking for us.

At the time, we were growing so fast and getting so big, I couldn't visit our stores as often as I used to, but I still stopped in regularly. On a particular Saturday afternoon, I made a visit to the Best Buy on South Robert Street in West St. Paul to see how things were going. I spent an hour in the store and then got in the car, planning to head home for dinner.

Sandy and I tried to eat together every night when I was in town, although we weren't often alone. Sandy was well known for her warm hospitality and for the hot dish that could always stretch to accommodate last-minute business guests. The kids were growing up fast—my youngest was about seventeen, and the two oldest were out of the house. Susan, my oldest daughter, had graduated with a communications degree from the University of Minnesota that spring and was working with Best Buy in the Investor Relations and Public Relations department.

As I've said, in order to keep costs down, we didn't locate Best Buy stores in the big shopping malls in those days. But we always sited them *close* to a mall, so we could benefit from the customer traffic. The South Robert Street store was near the Signal Hills Shopping Center, a local mall with a mix of businesses, including a regional department store and a family restaurant. As I drove past the complex on my way home, I noted that things looked slow there. Maybe ten cars in the parking lot.

I drove south, heading for Highway 494, and in a few blocks passed another shopping center. A Sam's Club, the warehouse-style, deep-discount operation of Wal-Mart, had just opened there. I glanced over and couldn't believe my eyes. The parking lot was packed—hardly a space to be had. People were streaming out the front door, their carts and baskets overflowing with goods. They looked downright excited.

I had to check this out. I turned into the lot and circled around until I found a space. I sat in the car and watched the action for a while. It was amazing. The flow of traffic in and out of the store did not let up. The people entering looked as if they couldn't wait to get inside. The people exiting were jabbering away as if they'd never had so much fun. Their carts were piled high with all kinds of goods, including groceries, clothing, and plenty of consumer electronics—many of the same items we offered at Best Buy. What's more, these shoppers didn't seem to fit any standard demographic. You had well-dressed, middle-aged women loading up their Mercedes, young couples in convertibles, families in station wagons, young guys in pickup trucks, and seniors in Cadillacs. And they all looked victorious!

I said to myself, *I need to understand this phenomenon a whole lot better.* So I went inside.

I found myself in the middle of an absolute circus.

I signed up and paid my fee—I think it was $25—and joined the crowd. The aisles were clogged with people and carts. The assortment was huge and the prices unbelievably low. There was nothing fancy about the atmosphere, but it was exciting and lively. No one was trying to sell anyone anything, but customers were buying everything. I wandered around for twenty minutes or so without making a purchase, but feeling the urge to buy a lot.

I drove home thinking about our competitive situation. Sure, we were doing everything we could to prevail against Highland. But even if we beat them, who would be after us next? Circuit City? They were much bigger than we were. And how long would it be before Sam's Club and Wal-Mart were selling our brands of consumer electronics, too?

I reminded myself to listen to the customer. What exactly were the customers saying at Sam's Club? Yes, they were saying they liked low prices. And, yes, they were saying they enjoyed an exciting, low-pressure environment. But I thought they were really saying something much more fundamental and important. I heard customers saying, *We want to be in control!*

Could that be the secret? If we gave customers more control, would that help us beat Highland? And Circuit City? And everybody else?

There was only one way to find out.

CHAPTER SEVEN

A GAME
CHANGER

Concept II

HOW COULD WE GIVE THE CUSTOMER MORE CONTROL? And if we found a way to give them more control, what would that mean for us? How would a new retailing model change our company? How would it affect our people?

I would like to say that I knew the answers to these questions back in 1986, but I didn't. What I did know was that we were in a different situation than we ever had been before. Yes, we had been in tough spots. We had come close to bankruptcy—twice. We'd been whacked by a tornado. We had been at the mercy of our suppliers.

But now, in our struggle with Highland, we were being *attacked*. I can hardly describe what that feels like. It's one thing to compete fairly with another company. To differentiate yourself from them. To define your market position and your customers. To play fair. It's quite another to have a much larger company enter your market with the express intention of driving you out of business. Setting up shop right across the street. Advertising in your face. Selling at totally unrealistic and unsustainable prices. If Highland had succeeded in putting us out of business, do you think it would have continued to sell products at such low prices? Not a chance. It was a con on the customer—a classic example of Highland leveraging its profitable markets to capture ours.

Why did the Mondrys care so much about Minneapolis? Why was it necessary for them to target Best Buy? What was driving them? Were they afraid of us as competition? Offended by our ambitions? Jealous of our growth? Probably it was all of those things. Certainly, their attitude was very different from that of any other competitor we faced. Circuit City didn't attack us in the way Highland did. Nor had Schaak or Team Electronics.

Whatever was driving the Mondrys, it ultimately had the opposite effect from the one they expected. Instead of slowing our growth or killing us, Highland's move to the Twin Cities set the stage for its own derailment.

That's largely because the Mondrys expected us to keep playing the game the way it had always been played. But I saw that, in order to win against Highland, we had to change the playing field. We needed a transformation . . . a paradigm shift . . . a disruption. We needed to make Highland look like the horse and buggy, as we whizzed past them like a brand-new, fast-paced automobile.

Fortunately, we found just such a breakthrough. And apart from the shift from Sound of Music to Best Buy, it was the most important thing we have ever done. It was a seminal move that changed our industry.

We called it *Concept II*.

THINKING THE UNTHINKABLE

As I have said before, I am not a visionary. Concept II did not come to me in a dream. It evolved out of many conversations we had about how we could improve the Best Buy customer experience. Could we somehow re-create the excitement of the tornado sale? Could we capture some of the feeling of a warehouse club? Should we provide more information? Can we create a better environment in the store? What would improve our service after purchase?

Inevitably, the conversations led to one topic: directed selling. The entire consumer electronics industry had been built around incentives and commissions. The suppliers exerted control over the retailers through spiffs. Retailers exerted control over the customer through incentives, such as discounts and rebates, as well as directed selling. If we wanted to give the customer more control and a better store experience, we could never do it in a sales-directed environment. We needed to depressurize the experience.

All of this brought us to one question. It was almost heresy to ask it, let alone think it: *Could we* abolish *commissions?*

That idea doesn't sound very earth-shattering now. But you have to understand how entrenched the practice was then. In 1986, of our one thousand employees, more than half worked on commission—almost six hundred. Many of them had been with the company for years, some for twenty years. They had shaped their careers and lifestyles around commissioned sales. They had built their lives on the income they had been able to generate through commissions. Everybody knew how the process worked, and everybody accepted it. They had spent years learning the trade and getting good at it.

What's more, we had always had very good relations with our employees, and we worked hard to keep it that way. Maybe we didn't have the small, family atmosphere that we had enjoyed when we were Sound of Music, but Best Buy still had a strong company spirit. I didn't want to put that in jeopardy.

Going to a noncommissioned sales model would be risky. We could easily lose many of our salespeople. Sure, we could hire new employees to replace them. But how long would it take to train them? Would they be able to offer the kind of experience we were trying to create? Would getting rid of commissions cause a lot of disruption in the stores? Might the disruption turn customers off?

The more I thought about it, though, the more obvious it became that the noncommissioned approach could be a game changer for the industry. More and more of the big retail chains were getting into consumer electronics, and we would soon face increasing competition from them. Most deep-discount stores, like Sam's Club, didn't pay commissions. Plus, Highland was a commissioned model, and so were the other consumer electronics chains. If we moved away from commissions, that could be a very powerful differentiator for us, a significant cost benefit.

I got the board involved in the discussion. At last, we agreed on a plan. We would test the noncommission strategy gradually. We'd start with a limited number of stores, and they would be located in smaller markets outside the Twin Cities. In each market, we would identify a number of salespeople who had the potential to be managers. They would be promoted and paid a salary with incentive opportunities. The remaining salespeople would be paid on an hourly basis.

In the new stores, the salespeople would play a different role than they had before. The salesperson would be thought of as a facilitator. He or she would provide information and would be available to give advice and make recommendations. Salespeople would still help customers, but only when customers wanted help. Otherwise, they would greet and welcome customers—and leave them alone when they wanted to be left alone.

We knew that the noncommission model would have positives and negatives for the salespeople. The compensation would be different. The managers would earn a higher base salary than they had when they were salespeople working on commission, but the ones who had made a lot of money on commissions would certainly earn less than before. Although most employees would be eligible for bonuses, these would be based on the performance of the entire store or district rather than on individual success.

There were some important benefits that might outweigh the lower compensation. The salespeople who chose to become managers could move up through the Best Buy system. They could move from store to store. They could run a district or a region. They might end up expanding their special talent at headquarters. The bigger we got, and the more we expanded, the more opportunities there were. So we had actually opened up a fast-paced career path for lots of people. And over the years, Best Buy has made a point of promoting from within. I started out in the stores. So did Brad and Brian. But for those who were interested only in their own benefit and weren't interested in management, the new system might not be so attractive.

For the customer, however, the move to noncommission could only be good. There would be no more spiffs. No more secret handshakes between salespeople and warehouse pickers. Much less pressure to buy. Greater freedom to choose among a wider range of products. Much more transparency about price and availability. *The customer would have a whole lot more control.*

We realized that we couldn't abolish commissions without changing the way we handled inventory and stock. In order to give the customer the most control, *all* the store's inventory would have to be right there, on the floor, in plain view. If the customer knew what he wanted, he could grab it and go. If he wanted to talk about features and benefits of different models in detail, a salesperson would be available to do so. The product demonstrations would not be biased toward any one brand, and the customer would have plenty of opportunity to compare brands, models, and features.

We didn't stop there. At Elliot Kaplan's suggestion, a new director had joined us a year earlier, and he helped us push Concept

II even further. Richard N. Cardozo was a professor of strategic management and organization at the Carlson School of Management at
the University of Minnesota. Richard held a bachelor's degree in psychology, an MBA from Harvard Business School, and a PhD in business administration from Minnesota. In other words, he had more
college degrees than Al, Brad, Zeke, and I had put together.

Professor Cardozo was particularly interested in the look and
feel of the new stores. "Forget about carpeting," he said. "Let's go
with cement floors! Let's lose the wooden display shelves and cases.
Instead, we'll have metal racks. Let's not waste money on printed
signs with the product names and prices. Handwritten signs on cardboard will do. And all that spotlighting? Not necessary. It sends the
wrong message. Fluorescent lighting is all we need."

"Customers don't care about how things look," Richard said.
"They want assortment. Selection. They want good service and
friendly people. But most of all, they want low prices. So everything
about the environment should scream, *Best Buy means great value!*"

The professor thought we were onto something very big. He
thought the new model would make Highland look like a relic from the
1930s. What's more, he thought it could change the face of consumer
electronics retailing across the country—maybe even the world.

Who was I to argue with a learned academic?

WE PLACE OUR BET

We decided to test Concept II in seven new locations: Champaign,
Rockford, Bloomington, and Springfield, Illinois; Wichita and
Topeka, Kansas; and Lincoln, Nebraska. We'd open the stores
starting in the spring of 1988. We'd give them a year or so. If Concept
II worked in those stores, we'd roll it out to all the rest. If it didn't
work . . . Well, I was determined to *make* it work.

So, in advance of the Concept II launch, we developed and refined the format over a period of about eighteen months. We specified the new store layout. We redesigned our inventory management process. We tinkered with product assortment.

We also started talking with our suppliers, working hard to sell them on Concept II. By now I hope it's clear that supplier relationships are a critical part of consumer electronics retailing. If the suppliers didn't like Concept II, they might terminate our contract and stop deliveries. At the time, we weren't big enough to make any ultimatums. The big suppliers could sever ties with us and hardly feel a pinch. There were plenty of other outlets for them to sell through.

So, we put a lot of effort into explaining the new concept to our suppliers. Most of them went along with the idea, but some of them hated it. Cement floors? Fluorescent lighting? Products stacked in their boxes? No commissions? *This doesn't feel right*, they'd say. *We're not selling canned corn or paper towels. We make high-quality products. They deserve better than this.* The lesser-known, higher-end brands disliked Concept II the most. We lost component suppliers Onkyo and Mitsubishi, and we almost lost JVC; we lost a number of appliance suppliers, too. In all, a half dozen suppliers said they didn't want their lines in the new stores—or in our other ones, either. That would hurt, but we felt we could survive and prove our concept was the right one for most customers. We were fortunate to have the support of Harry Elias of JVC. He stood by us and convinced many suppliers who were on the fence to give our strategy a chance. To this day, we appreciate Harry's efforts on our behalf.

While we were developing Concept II, we were also opening new stores at a rapid pace. In 1988, we opened sixteen superstores and entered two big new markets for us: St. Louis and Kansas City, Missouri. In 1989, we opened another five stores. We had thirty more in various stages of planning and development. We were hiring and training hundreds of new people each year. We had big plans. We were impatient. We saw a huge opportunity. And we fully intended to seize the day!

We didn't want Concept II to jeopardize the good thing we had going. To convert an existing store required closing it for a while. That meant losing revenue in the short term. It could mean losing market share in the long term as well. We also wanted to incorporate Concept II into the new stores, if it worked. So we wanted to get results from the idea as fast as possible.

In other words, we were facing a classic business problem. We were trying to make a big change to a rapidly growing business, which is pretty much like trying to change a tire while you're driving at a hundred miles an hour. You have to do it, but it's really dangerous. We knew that expanding too fast or investing too heavily in the wrong products or wrong format could, in fact, kill us. After all, we had seen Schaak and Team Electronics and others struggle and then go out of business.

We were often criticized by analysts and the press for our ambitious plans, and I have to admit there was some cause for their concern. The problem was profit. Although our revenue was growing fast, our profits were actually declining. The revenue picture was pretty rosy. We grew from $239 million in 1987, to $439 million 1988, to $507 million in 1989. The profit picture was not so pretty. We earned $7.7 million in 1987, $2.8 million in 1988, and $2.1 million in 1989. Wall Street loves growth, but it likes profit right along with the sales growth: *Sure, Best Buy can build the top line by opening new stores like crazy. But can it actually make any money?*

There were many factors contributing to our profit decline. The economy was a little shaky. But the main reason was that our customers knew a great deal about technology and the products we sold. They bought the lowest-margin products on the sales floor, and without upgrades and add-ons, our profits were low. There was simply not enough margin to leverage our cost of sales.

What we didn't realize completely at the time was that Highland was struggling with its own issues and was, in fact, in deep trouble. The company had expanded much too aggressively and had taken on far too much debt to do so. In the four-year period from 1985 to 1989, Highland more than doubled its number of stores—growing from forty locations to eighty-four. In 1989, although Best Buy made only a bit more than $2 million in profit, Highland *lost* $12.3 million. In the first quarter of 1990, the company lost another $2.7 million. Its share price plunged. Highland couldn't keep going like that for very long.

So we forged ahead with Concept II. We opened the seven test stores and, soon enough, we began to see some encouraging results. Sales in the new-format stores moved ahead of those in stores with the old commission format. I'm not saying it was an instant hit. In fact, it took years to fully realize the benefits of Concept II. But the model had enough potential that we decided to start rolling it out to other locations. Maybe Concept II was the future of Best Buy, and maybe even the future of the industry. And of course, that's exactly what it proved to be.

As word got out about our new format, we watched as the Highland stores tried to copy it. They stacked merchandise on the showroom floor and installed information kiosks. But it was a half-hearted attempt. I began to smell defeat in the air. And it wasn't ours.

JOHN HENRY (A.K.A. BRIAN DUNN) FIGHTS THE STEAM SHOVEL

As we gained experience with Concept II, we made adjustments and refinements. We softened up the warehouse look a bit. We wanted to give the impression that Best Buy offered good value, but we didn't have to look downright *cheap*. We allowed the salespeople to assert themselves a little more. We found that, yes, the customer wants control, but the customer also wants guidance and help. We searched for the right formula.

We also began to prepare people throughout the company for the day that their store would convert to Concept II. Many of them resisted. One of them was Brian Dunn. Since battling bravely against the Highland invasion as assistant manager of the Minnetonka store, Brian had gotten a big promotion. He became manager at the Edina store in 1989. He was delighted. Here's how he remembers his new position:

> *"I was honored. I had surpassed my wildest expectations. I loved running a commissioned sales staff. I loved the day-to-day work with 150 people, watching them grow and develop. Building teams was very, very satisfying to me. I loved the company that had given me this great opportunity to lead. I would have been thrilled to run the store for the next fifteen years."*

Well, Brian didn't get to run Edina for fifteen years. In fact, he barely got to manage it for a year. Just thirteen months after that promotion, Brian got an even bigger one. His boss asked him to become a district manager. He said, "Thanks, but no thanks."

His boss asked him again.

Brian said, "I mean it. I love running a store. I don't want to be a district manager."

Finally, I had a little talk with him. I said, "Brian, I know you love what you're doing. You're good at it. Wouldn't it be great if you could do what you're doing for many *more* people than you have now?'" This opened his eyes. It was one of those offers you can't really refuse.

Brian Dunn in his store management days.

So Brian took over District I in 1990 and found himself even more embroiled in the Highland fight. District I comprised seven stores, including Edina, Burnsville, and Ridgedale. District II had five stores. The two city districts had always been more or less friendly competitors. Each month, they would try to beat the pants off each other in terms of sales. But when Highland came to town, District I and District II united against the common enemy.

Brian would get all the Twin Cities store managers together regularly. Sometimes they'd meet early in the morning over coffee or breakfast at the local pancake house. They'd discuss the day's plans and share news of Highland's latest moves. Other days they would gather at 10:00 P.M. to review the events of the day: *What have we learned? How's it going? What's selling? What's not?*

Brian also had to contend with Concept II. District I was still on commission and Brian and his salespeople had no interest in converting to the new format. They did everything they could to bump up revenue and improve profits. They thought: *We have to beat this thing or we're going to lose our jobs!*

Then one day Brian decided it was time to get a firsthand look at the fast-growing Concept II in action. Remember: *know your competition!* Brian had heard a lot about Concept II, but he hadn't visited one of our new stores. So one day, on an impulse, he rented a Winnebago. He grabbed six of his managers. They drove three hundred miles to the closest Concept II location—Rockford, Illinois. Even though they hadn't been invited to the store, they barged right in and spent a couple of hours observing.

At the end of the visit, Brian realized that he was like John Henry with his hammer, trying to beat the steam shovel. Concept II was the new thing. Brian didn't love everything about it, but he saw that it was the future. We had already begun rolling out the format beyond the original seven Concept II stores. Brian knew he would eventually get the call saying it was time to "flip the switch" in his district.

Brian decided he had to get ready for the inevitable. He prepared a list of fifty people he would invite to join the manager training program. The others would be asked to go on hourly compensation. Brian would try to grandfather the salaries of some of the more senior people. But many people would face a cut of 25 to 30 percent in their compensation. Brian knew how much that could hurt, because he had gone through it himself when he became assistant store manager. (In fact, Brian's wife, Sue, had told him he was crazy to take the promotion!)

One Sunday afternoon, Brian got the word that it was time to flip the switch. He spent the evening on the phone with his sales staff. About half the people he talked to agreed to stay on. The other half said no. Many of those were talented people who had made important contributions to the company. It was tough to say good-bye to them. As Brian said, "One of the things we should be really proud of is that Best Buy taught those people how to sell. They were really grateful for the experience they had here."

HIGHLAND RETREATS AND WE GIVE CHASE

The battle continued. We were holding our own, but we couldn't be sure how long we could withstand the Highland onslaught. And then, all of a sudden, the enemy retreated!

In May 1990, Highland closed its stores in Milwaukee. Ninety-five people lost their jobs there. Gene Mondry was quoted in an article in the *Milwaukee Sentinel*, saying, "We could have kept the stores open—we have never dropped out of a marketplace before—but we decided not to make an emotional decision. We had to look at it in the broad context. We wanted to concentrate on our core markets, and Milwaukee is just not a strong market for us. So, we decided to get out."

Riiiiiight!

At the same time, Highland cancelled plans to open new stores in New York state. No, the company wasn't exactly finished. It still operated eighty-nine stores and had a presence in ten states. But it wasn't exactly on the attack anymore.

Highland hung on for another year in Minneapolis. But all the news about the company was bad, and we knew it was just a matter of time before the Mondrys called it quits. In the winter of 1991, we began hearing the rumors: *Highland is pulling out of the Twin Cities.* From the original three stores opened in 1987, it had expanded to six. We estimated Highland was taking in around $45 million with those six stores, while we were doing around $140 million with our ten locations. So we were taking in almost twice as much revenue per store as Highland was. Do the math. Highland wasn't doing enough volume or making enough profit. It hadn't built a customer base or created customer loyalty. The simple fact was that

A Highland sign is dismantled.

customers preferred the Best Buy experience.

On Wednesday, April 3, 1991, Highland closed all six of its stores in the Twin Cities area. On Friday, April 5, the stores reopened for a going-out-of-business sale. Two hundred people were put out of work. An article appearing in the *Star Tribune* opened as follows:

It is only right and just that we write this day to commemorate the exodus of Highland superstores from our not-always-fair environs. After a four-year slugfest between the Detroit-based electronic retailer and Bloomington-based Best Buy Inc., the hometown boys have beaten the Highland guys in Minneapolis, having forced them out of Milwaukee just last year.

Highland was in much more serious trouble than the closing of the Twin Cities stores seemed to indicate. As it withdrew from Minneapolis, Highland also closed existing stores in New York. The company announced that it would take a restructuring charge of at least $9 million. And that it was looking for a buyer for its remaining eighty-two stores.

How did I feel about our victory? I felt like doing something I rarely did. Something I still don't do very often. I felt like spending money on a celebration. People who know me will tell you that is not my normal character. But come on! We had just emerged as the winner in a long contest with the country's second-largest player in

The management team celebrates Highland's retreat from the Twin Cities.

the industry—a company that had been trying to take us down. Not only had we routed them from our turf, we had struck a blow that might ultimately prove fatal to them.

I do not consider myself a vindictive or mean person. But Highland had deliberately attacked the business we had been building for twenty-five years. The company had tried to destroy us with brutal tactics that, in the end, were self-defeating. It had put the thousands of people who worked for Best Buy in jeopardy.

The right thing to do was celebrate! So we threw a party.

On Saturday, April 27, Best Buy people swarmed into the ballroom at the Hyatt Regency in downtown Minneapolis. All the gentlemen were decked out in tuxedos. The ladies wore their finest long gowns. We danced to live music. We sipped champagne. We feasted on a five-course dinner.

After the meal I offered a few remarks. I'll admit that I was pretty

revved up. I said that, together, we had achieved an exceptional outcome. Not only had we beaten Highland at its own game, we had
completely changed the playing field with Concept II. And now it
was time for a little quid pro quo. Highland had come after us, now
we would go after them. It wasn't enough for us to force Highland
out of the Twin Cities. We were going to chase them. We were going
to run them out of every city where they were most vulnerable. We'd
confront them in Dallas . . . Houston . . . Indianapolis.

But, as I told the ballroom full of our people, even that wasn't
enough. I wanted to challenge Highland where the company really
lived. That meant going to one of its most precious markets, Chicago.
And then marching right onto Highland's home turf: Detroit. The
crowd went wild.

I won't tell you what that evening cost. (I think I've blocked it
out of my memory.) But I know it was worth every penny.

A LITTLE GLITCH IN CHICAGO

On November 19, 1991, we made the announcement: Best Buy would
open fifteen to eighteen stores in the greater Chicago area in the following twelve months. We were getting pretty good at opening stores
quickly. We were also quite successful at raising money to fund our
expansions. In October, we closed an offering of 2.5 million shares
of common stock at $31.25 per share. This time we went out on the
road with Goldman Sachs in our corner. Subscription was enthusiastic. We were up to seventy-four stores, two-thirds of which were
operating with the Concept II model. Our growth prospects looked
very good.

Going into an established market like Chicago, however, was
quite a different undertaking from opening a store where there was
essentially no competition. We knew Chicago wouldn't be easy. Not

only was Highland well entrenched there, but we'd be facing a slew of other competitors, including Sears, Fretter, Silo, and Montgomery Ward. We'd also be competing with several stores that primarily sold music. (One of them would become very important to us in just a few years: Musicland. But that's a story for a later chapter.) Plus, the economy still wasn't doing particularly well. What's more, the electronics retailers were looking for the next hot product. The VCR was essentially dead, and the CD player hadn't taken off yet. The entire industry was in a bit of a funk.

The opening of our first Chicago stores was set for September 11, 1992. The press was buzzing: *Best Buy is coming to Chicago!* The financial communities were talking us up. Just as we were putting the finishing touches on plans for the grand opening, however, we got a disturbing phone call from one of our key suppliers, a major national brand that is still an important and valued supplier to us.

"We need to talk with you." It was the president of the supplier's North America operation.

"What about?" I asked.

"I can't tell you over the phone. You have to come to New York. We need a meeting."

"This doesn't sound good," Brad said when I told him. He looked worried. "It must be about Chicago."

Brad and I flew to New York. We sat down to dinner with two executives from the supplier—which was one of our largest at the time.

"We've done a study in Chicago," one of them said. "We've come to the conclusion that our brand has adequate market share in that market."

"Really?" I said. *Adequate* market share? What supplier ever thinks it has *adequate* market share? Something fishy was going on.

"Yes," said the rep. "So we have decided that we are *not* going to authorize Best Buy to sell our products in Chicago."

I couldn't believe what I was hearing. I took a deep breath and tried to control my temper. "Let me get this straight," I said. "You're not going to authorize us to sell your products in our Chicago stores?"

"That's correct," said the rep.

"Because you have *adequate* market share in Chicago. You wouldn't want to have any more market share?"

The rep ignored that one. "Of course, we're happy with our relationship with Best Buy everywhere else. Don't worry. It's just Chicago." He smiled.

This was not good news. Our grand opening was in three weeks. This supplier's products were integrated into the mix of categories. We had their merchandise in stock. The ads were all ready to run.

"Hmm," I said. "And that's your final decision?"

"Yes, that's our final decision," he said.

I was beyond angry. I was livid. I was convinced I knew exactly why the brand was pulling out. In my opinion, it had nothing to do with studies or market share. It had everything to do with two competitors: Sears and Montgomery Ward. Both were headquartered in Chicago. Both were big national chains with lots of clout. Once again, the big boys were after us.

In my mind, I could hear the Sears buyer talking to the supplier's rep. *Listen*, the Sears guy would have said, *we sell your product in a thousand stores all over the United States. We've supported you and your brand for years. Now this upstart, Best Buy, is coming to Chicago. All these guys care about is price. They're going to upset the market. We don't want Best Buy selling your brand in our home city. If you let them carry it, we won't carry it. Simple as that.*

Brad had a minor freak-out. "Without that brand, we can't possibly succeed in Chicago," he said. "That's a major seller! It must be fifteen percent of our business in the most important categories.

Customers ask for it by name. What are we going to do? We'll be out of business before we even open our doors!"

When I'm mad, I get even more determined than usual. "No, we won't," I said. "We've got three weeks. Here's what we're going to do. We're going to contact every secondary and tertiary brand we sell. They're all good brands: Sanyo, Sharp, Quasar, Motorola, Magnavox, Toshiba, Hatachi. They don't have the name recognition, but they make fine products. We're going to buy more merchandise from them. We're going to get their best equivalents of the products we've lost. We're not going to apologize or explain. We're going to stock up our shelves like these are the greatest products going. And we're going to build a market for all of them."

The very next day we started working the phones. We said to the suppliers, "Look, we want to open our Chicago stores with your products. We want to showcase your brand. We want to put you on the map in the city of Chicago. We think we can build a strong following for your products here and throughout our system." They all agreed.

We were ready to go on opening day. We stacked the shelves high with great products. We priced them right. We emphasized that even if the customer didn't recognize the brand names, these were good products at great values. In fact, we managed to turn the lack of that major brand into a positive thing—for Best Buy and for our customers.

It took everyone working together to save the day. Here's how Tim Sheehan—who is now Chief Administration Officer and Enterprise Executive Vice President—remembers it:

"We leaped many hurdles to get the Chicago market off the ground. The number one brand, the one with the most enviable position in the consumer electronics marketplace, elected not to support our entry into the Chicago market for what they said were 'strategic reasons.' This was a shock to us.

Leadership was frustrated and the store teams were worried. How would we tell the new Chicago customers that we didn't have the leading brand in stock?

Well, we decided to turn the snub into a rallying cry. We dissected our product assortment and came up with an alternative-brand product for every SKU we were missing from the big brand. We trained our people extra hard on those SKUs. Instead of feeling sorry for ourselves, we said, 'Hey, who needs them when we have Sharp and all these other great brands?' But we never bad-mouthed the absent brand to our customers. In fact, our sales teams demonstrated amazing respect and integrity. They tactfully explained that, yes, we were doing business with the leading brand in other markets, but not in Chicago. And they showed customers that there were quality alternatives that could deliver just what they wanted.

Then we closely monitored sales performance. When all was said and done, we proved that we could have a major impact in the Chicago market without the number one brand."

As Tim says, our strategy worked. In fact, it worked beyond our wildest dreams. We sold those alternative-brand products to the wall! In just five weeks, thanks to our skyrocketing sales in Chicago, there was a 3 percent shift in market share. That was a huge, fast drop for the supplier that had removed its products from our Chicago stores. I guess the folks there didn't consider their share to be quite so adequate anymore: Months later, in January, we bumped into the reps at the Consumer Electronics Show in Las Vegas—the same guys we had had dinner with in New York.

"Hey, we've done another review of the market," one of them said. "We've determined that we'd like to come back in with you."

"Oh, really? What changed?" I asked.

He just smiled.

By March, the big-name brand was back on our shelves, as if it had never left. That episode taught us an important lesson: *Customers will always respond to real value, whatever the brand.* All you have to do is show them a good quality product that works well at an extraordinary price and back it with excellent service.

I should note, however, that the Chicago opening came at a cost. It put a lot of strain on our people. Here's how Tim describes that experience:

> *"Entering Chicago was a wild ride, unlike any other in my twenty-five-year career. The odds seemed stacked against us. Nobody was sure how it would all work out. But we committed ourselves to winning the market and staying the course.*
>
> *However, I witnessed a lot of sacrifices. People uprooting their families in pursuit of a new challenge or future promotion. People spending countless hours away from spouses and kids. Marriages broken up because the demands of relationship and career got too far out of whack. Disappointment and frustration when team members could not rise to the challenge and had to take a demotion or go back home.*
>
> *When we could help people through the challenges and watch them grow, it was extremely rewarding. When it didn't go well, and we were unable to help, it was tough to watch."*

I include Tim's comments even though they are painful to read. I simply want to thank everyone for their incredible contributions to the Chicago effort and to express my sympathies for those whose lives or careers suffered as part of the process. It is impossible for a large company to move forward, take risks, and win battles without some people being negatively affected by the struggle. I hope that for the great majority of Best Buy employees, however, the results have been well worth the fight!

AN OFFER I COULD EASILY REFUSE

Before we could take the fight to Highland in Chicago, the company retreated once again, closing all its Chicago stores before we could open even one of ours. An article in *Billboard* magazine told the story:

> *Highland Superstores filed for protection under Chapter 11 of the U.S. bankruptcy laws Aug. 25 and announced it would pull out of Chicago. The chain began liquidating its stock 2½ weeks before Best Buy opened its first eight stores. Many observers correlate the Highland flight from the Chicago market with Best Buy's entry here.*

After its exit from Chicago, Highland quickly fell apart. The company filed a reorganization plan that summer, but it was rejected by the stores' creditors. On March 16, 1993, Highland announced that the company would liquidate its assets and cease all operations. Proceeds from the sale of assets would go to creditors. Shareholders would get nothing.

One day we got a call from Gene Mondry, one that I'm sure he never expected to make. The Mondrys wanted to sit down with us. They would like us to consider acquiring some of the company assets. Would we come to Detroit for a meeting?

We met at the airport—Brad, Elliot, Gene and Ira Mondry, and I.

Highland eventually lost it all.

They made their pitch. They didn't seem to accept that their company was on the road to extinction. They were as arrogant as ever. They said that they knew we were considering entering the Detroit market. They could offer us some good advice about how to compete there. They would sell us their warehouse and a few other properties and assets at a fire-sale price.

We listened. I asked if they would excuse us for a few moments so we could talk it over. *Sure,* was the answer. *Take your time.* We went into the hall and closed the door behind us.

"Elliot," I said, "hell will be frozen over and the devil will be skating on it before I give them a dime."

As Elliot puts it now, "We went back in with our offer. Nothing. They didn't take it. Then we walked out."

At least they didn't refer to Brad as "son."

THE VALUES BEHIND THE NUMBERS

Concept II worked. In fact, it was the most seminal moment in our company's history, even though it wasn't exactly a moment at all. In fact it took six years, from 1990 to 1996, to roll out and perfect the new format throughout the Best Buy system.

Concept II worked because we never took our eyes off its main purpose: to provide added benefit to the customer. The customer was our most important consideration, followed by our employees, our shareholders, and our suppliers. We believed that if we served the customers well (and gave them consistently great values), all the other stakeholders would benefit, too.

It was hard to argue with the results we achieved with Concept II. Our parking lots filled with customers. Our volume grew, and our revenue climbed. Before Concept II, the average volume of a com- mission-format store was about $12 million. With Concept II, it shot up to $28 million per store. Our little profit problem also seemed to have been solved. After reaching a low of $2.1 million profit in 1989, we made $5.6 million in 1990 and nearly $10 million in 1992.

The new approach rippled through the entire industry. Everyone took notice, including Wall Street. East Coast analysts continued to make the trek to the unfamiliar Midwest to see what was going on with this company called Best Buy.

I personally witnessed one analyst's method of evaluation when, one day, I happened to be visiting the Concept II store in Rockford. I was walking past the checkout when I noticed a fellow in line with a cart absolutely chock-full of merchandise. He looked a bit out of place: It was the middle of the day, and the store was mostly filled with moms, kids, twentysomethings, and seniors. This guy was wearing a business suit and tie. When I looked more closely at him, I realized I knew him. It was Skip Helm, an analyst for William Blair

& Company, an old-line investment firm based in Chicago and one of our underwriters.

I went over and said, "Hi."

Skip looked a bit sheepish. He told me that he'd come on business, but when he saw the great stuff and the low prices, he couldn't *not* buy something.

How great was that? The chairman of the company, walking the floor, sees the analyst in line with a basket of goodies. I figured we'd get a good write-up. And we did.

But Concept II was not just about financial performance. That period of transition and rapid growth also made us recognize the importance of values to our success.

Today, we have stated our values clearly, and everybody in the company is exposed to them and knows what they are. I'll discuss these values in depth in Chapter Eleven. There are only four of them, and they're pretty simple:

- Have fun while being the best.
- Learn from challenge and change.
- Show respect, humility, and integrity.
- Unleash the power of our people.

Back in the early 1990s, however, our company values weren't so out in the open. Yes, I believed in them. I tried to live them every day. So did Brad and Al and the other members of the management team. But we were growing so fast, we couldn't interact with everybody directly anymore. Although most of the new people shared our values, we found that some didn't. When a store manager operated with different values, that's what the employees saw. And they believed those were the company's values.

It was during this period of intense change and rapid growth that we began to realize something that probably should have been very obvious. While we at the top of the company hierarchy lived by a set of core values, we had not clearly embedded them throughout the organization. An essential role for managers is to live the company's values themselves and to ensure that others do, too. We saw that we couldn't just sit back and expect all our managers and thousands of Best Buy employees to know and live our values. We had to make our values explicit. We had to talk about them. We had to *keep* talking about them.

It was in those years that Brad and I began paying closer attention to who was living the values and who was not. If we felt that someone was not performing in a way consistent with our core values, we'd have an honest conversation with that person. Brad was particularly attentive to the values and very good at those conversations.

In other words, it was during those years that we began to really learn what *management* and corporate leadership were all about. Remember, none of us had any formal grounding in the art or science of management. We were retail guys. We had always been focused on operations: purchasing . . . inventory . . . store openings . . . staffing . . . controlling costs. We were making up our management approach as we went along. We had to learn the disciplines, routines, and skills involved in managing a large organization and creating a national brand at the same time.

It wasn't easy. I'm still learning every day.

ONE BILLION AND COUNTING

As I worked on this book, my colleagues warned me to be careful of engaging in what they call "euphoric recall." That means remembering things through rose-colored glasses. Here's how Brian puts it:

"We have to fight the notion that you have a flash of brilliance when you get a strategy. Then you execute it and make tons of money. No. You get an idea, which is often borne out of desperation. Then you go out and work it with tenacity. You fail fast. You iterate and iterate and iterate. With Concept II, we learned that the noncommission, no-pressure environment helped us. But we also learned that we had to have some salesmanship, too. We had to sell warranties, accessories, service, peripherals, financing, and everything else, or we weren't going to make any money. Once we merged those seemingly paradoxical components, we had a model that worked really, really great."

That is very true. But the fact is that our new strategy did have some brilliance in it, even though it took a lot of hard work to execute properly. Some numbers help prove the point: In fiscal 1993, we hit a very significant financial milestone. We surpassed $1 billion in sales for the first time. The exact number, for the record, was actually $1,619,978,000. That was a *74 percent* increase from the previous year.

I was so excited that I decided, for the second time in three years, that we had to do something to celebrate. No black-tie banquet and live music this time, though. We ended up giving everybody—every single person in the company—a handsome blue jacket emblazoned with our logo and notice of this special milestone in our history. When my secretary, Donna, got hers, she said, "Wow, a billion dollars! I think this really is going to happen!" I guess she had her doubts up until that point.

We learned a very valuable lesson from Concept II: the importance of innovation. By setting our own course rather than following someone else's strategy, we earned recognition from our customers, shareholders, and suppliers. Innovation is also incredibly important to our employees. Not only do they see the value of the change, they also feel good about their role in making it successful.

Clearly, with Concept II, we were doing a lot of things right.

But as we soon discovered, we were also doing some very important things *completely wrong*. We were operating a $1 billion company in exactly the same way we had run it as a $50 million company. We knew that companies could go out of business by growing too fast or buying the wrong merchandise. What we didn't realize was that a company can also go under when its systems and processes can't stand the strain of growth. A company can almost literally break.

That was about to happen to us.

CHAPTER EIGHT

FAILURE IS NOT AN OPTION

I WISH I COULD SAY THAT I HAVE ALWAYS BEEN GOOD AT taking advice, but I can't. I did get better at listening to other people over the years, especially those who were in the Best Buy family. But I wasn't so keen on listening to outsiders. We preferred to promote from within, rather than hire senior people from the outside. We worked with plenty of subcontractors and suppliers, but we rarely hired consultants.

Whatever problems we had, I would think, *We should be able to figure this out by ourselves.*

That was standard operating procedure when we were Sound of Music. It worked for the first few years of Best Buy. But in 1990, we climbed aboard a rocket ship. It took off, and it was all we could do to hang on. We went from forty-nine stores in 1990 to 251 in 1996. In 1994 alone, we opened fifty-three stores—more than a store per week. We grew from 3,900 employees to 36,000, a tenfold increase. And from 1989 to 1996, revenue climbed from $512 million to well over *$7 billion.* Talk about scaling up!

With growth like that, it's no wonder cracks started to appear in the Best Buy ship. By the end of 1995, the whole thing was shaking violently. We were in danger of blowing up.

It's not surprising that we got to this point. After all, the skills of the entrepreneur—the drive and risk tolerance that enable a person to start a business from scratch—are quite different from those required to manage a large organization. Very few entrepreneurs make the transition from start-up leader to Fortune 500 CEO.

In addition to our operational issues, we had plenty of competition to contend with. Although we had defeated Highland, Circuit City was still out there and almost twice our size. As we got bigger and expanded nationally, they'd be gunning for us, too. We had to fix our organization, or we'd never be able to achieve the scale we needed to compete on the national (and later, international) stage.

To do so, I finally accepted that we didn't have the expertise we needed inside the company, although my colleagues had to drag me kicking and screaming to that realization. Two years after we brought in the outside experts, we were in better shape than we had ever been. That episode taught me some valuable lessons: You don't know everything. You *can't* know everything. There are some things you will never figure out by yourself, no matter how hard you try. There are good people out there, beyond the walls of your company. Open the door and let them in!

In other words, it's very important to *create strong partnerships*. It was a partnership that enabled us to achieve what has become known as the quickest turnaround in the history of retail. And it all started with a gigantic mistake.

THE COMPUTER DEBACLE

Computers gave us the wake-up call.

Computers had undone other consumer electronics firms. Schaak had bet on them big time, and it had killed the company.

In 1995, computers got us in trouble, too. In those days,

computers were not the commodities they are today. Every year, the manufacturers made them faster and smaller and added important new features. There were two main drivers of change: the processor and the operating system. Intel ruled the world of chips. Microsoft owned the operating system. (I'm not talking about Apple at the moment. They weren't nearly as important a player then as they became later.) Consumers naturally wanted to buy the very latest computer, the one with the most power, the greatest speed, and the most memory, at the lowest possible price. They paid close attention to what the manufacturers were doing. They knew when the next-generation processor or operating system would be released.

That made life very tough for the retailer. As soon as the new computer was announced, sales of the current one would start to drop. People would put off their purchase until the new one was available. Or they'd buy the current model, but only at the deepest discount they could find.

In 1995, everybody was waiting for the new operating system from Microsoft. The existing system, Windows 3.1, had been around since 1992. As early as 1993, Microsoft started talking about the next generation. But there were delays. The new system, Windows 95, was finally released to the industry in August 1995. That meant it would be available to the public in the first few months of 1996.

The timing could not have been worse for us. By August, we had already made our purchasing decisions for the upcoming holiday period. Computers accounted for about a third of our revenue, and some 80 percent of our total revenue came in during the period between Thanksgiving and the New Year.

We were expecting a big holiday season that year. Our computer buyer, Wayne Inouye, had loaded up on merchandise, well over *$1 billion* worth of inventory. In August, the trucks were already starting to roll in. We were committed. We were oh-so-committed.

We had taken on substantial debt to pay for that much inventory. Believe me, the suppliers weren't going to take it back.

Then it got worse. Intel announced it would also be introducing a new chip, optimized for running Windows 95. We knew the news was coming. I had even asked Intel to hold off on the announcement until after the holidays, but they ignored me.

Of course, Microsoft said, "Oh don't worry, the new operating system will run just fine on older chips." But consumers had heard that one before. Everybody knew that a next-generation operating system was always bigger and more complex than the earlier one. If you tried running Windows 95 on your old processor, you were asking for trouble.

Wayne heard the news before I did. He came to see me.

"Dick," he said, "I don't know how to tell you this, but we've got a problem."

"What is it?"

"I didn't do this intentionally."

"Do what intentionally?"

"We bought millions of computers for the holiday season."

"So?"

"They're obsolete."

Let me say right away that Wayne was not incompetent. In fact, he was a very skilled buyer. He made what he thought were the right decisions. We had supported him. But now he was a very unhappy camper.

Did I fire Wayne? No. He really understood the computer business and how to sell merchandise. He had built good relationships with our suppliers. Yes, he bought too many computers that year. But I couldn't put all the blame on him. Furthermore, Wayne had just gained an education (and a very expensive one) in the nature of the computer industry. If we gave him the boot, he'd land at some other company and put that education to work. Better that we should benefit from our own investment in his enlightenment! It was, of course, his responsibility to make sure he had learned the lesson and would act differently next time around—which I can assure you he did.

Besides, it was hardly the first time we'd had inventory troubles. Truth be told, the stores were always complaining: *I don't have enough inventory. I thought I was going to get X, and I got Y (or I didn't get anything)*. Our allocation system was pretty rudimentary. Say we got 250 units into a distribution center that served nine stores in Chicago. Divide 250 by nine. Each store would get twenty-seven units with a few left over. We didn't take into account how many units each individual store had sold in the past. We didn't forecast how many each individual store might sell in the future.

Because the stores were never sure what they would get, they would play games with ordering. If they thought they needed forty-eight television sets of a certain kind, they'd order one hundred, thinking, *Hey, HQ has been short-shipping us for years. We have to protect ourselves!* We were well aware of the issues. Brad (who was then president and chief operating officer), Wade Fenn (executive vice president of marketing), and the rest of the management team knew all about our problems. How could they not? The whining was profuse.

What did we do about our overstock of those obsolete computers? We decided that the first loss was the best loss. Starting in October, we reduced the price to our cost or below. By the time the holidays came around we had virtually nothing left to sell. We took a 25 percent haircut on our holiday revenue. What's more, our share price took a dive.

Not only did *we* get a haircut, the rest of the industry did, too. Selling that many computers at such low prices put pressure on all the other retailers. We weren't very popular that winter—except with our customers, who got some great deals on computers.

THE "YELLOW PAD" SUPPLY CHAIN

There was an upside to the "computer debacle," as we now call it. It gave us the wake-up call we needed. We realized we could not continue to use the same purchasing approach we had been using since the dawn of time.

In those days, we worked on four inventory turns per year. In other words, we'd order enough merchandise to last for a single quarter. Then we'd restock. But each product category actually turns over at a different rate from every other one. Today, we expect ten to twelve inventory turns for most fast-moving categories. Computers turn over twenty times a year, which means restocking every couple of weeks.

The computer debacle forced us to look carefully at how we were managing our supply chain—if you can call it "managing." The term *supply chain* refers to everything involved with getting products from the suppliers into the stores: the factories, the ships, the trucks, the warehouses, and all the systems and processes that keep track of everything. In 1995, we were operating out of a new head-quarters building located in Eden Prairie, a suburb a bit farther west of downtown Minneapolis. Our central warehouse was located in nearby Bloomington. We also had distribution centers in Oklahoma, Virginia, and California, and we were building a new one in Ohio. We bought goods from at least four hundred different manufacturers. Outside of the music and movie categories, we carried more than three thousand products, from refrigerators to computer cables. And each product might have several SKUs. An SKU, which means "stock keeping unit," refers to a variation on a basic product. There is a different SKU for each different color or different configuration of features, for example. There were significantly more variations available in software and music. We stocked sixty thousand CD titles alone, each with a different SKU number.

As you can imagine, we were constantly moving merchandise in and out of the warehouses and distribution centers and among the stores. Obviously, it would be impossible to juggle that many products without computerization. And over the years we had spent what I thought was a *lot* of money on computer systems. The problem was that we still had big gaps. One system kept track of purchasing: which products we bought, in what quantities, from which manufacturers. Another system kept track of distribution: what products went to which stores. But the two systems didn't talk to each other. To put it simply: the left hand didn't know what the right hand was doing.

As a result, we could not be certain as to what we had in stock. Five warehouses . . . tens of thousands of products . . . 251 stores. And no clue exactly what we could ship. No wonder Wayne bought too many computers. No wonder the store managers ordered more than they needed. They wanted to make sure they got *something*.

In the old days, when we were just in the Twin Cities, it was not unusual for a store manager to take inventory matters into his own hands. Brian did it many times when he was manager at the Edina store. Here's how he remembers it:

> *"When I was a store manager, the great curse was corporate voicemail. I'd be out of VCRs to sell. I'd call headquarters and get voicemail. My store was ten minutes down the road. I'd drive to the office. I'd interrupt a meeting to say, 'Hey, I know you guys are real busy, but I don't have any flipping VCRs to sell. Can somebody get me into the warehouse, please?' So they would. I would load up my Honda Accord with as many VCRs as I could, to tide us over. Then I'd send a pickup truck for more."*

Which brings me to the yellow pads.

We had another little problem with inventory. It was bad enough that we didn't know how *much* of any given item we had in stock. To make matters worse, we didn't know *where* it was in stock. And by "where" I don't mean which city—I mean which shelf. A truck would pull up with a delivery from a manufacturer. The stock handlers would unload the boxes and park them wherever they could find an empty space. If there was already stock of the same item on a different shelf, there was no effort to put the two quantities together.

Now, imagine you're a stock picker. You're the one who has to fulfill the orders from the stores. One of them needs a hundred CD players of a certain type—urgently! You know you have forty-eight on the shelf. You know that two hundred more were ordered from the supplier. But you don't know if they've come in or, if they have, where they might be. You don't have time to look around. You ship out the forty-eight you can find.

Nightmare! Our computerized information processing could not accurately keep up with our operational processing. We were like a jumbo aircraft flying at night without a navigation system. It was almost like we were flying blind.

Now put yourself in the shoes of the marketing person at headquarters. You have to decide what to feature in the weekly advertising insert. But you don't know which items we have in stock or how many we have of each. It got to the point that the only way to find out was to do what Brian did: Go to the warehouse. Walk from shelf to shelf. Count the boxes. Write down the numbers on a yellow pad.

One of the reasons this kind of practice persisted was that we had always valued the can-do attitude: If you have a problem, take action! Pitch in! Find a way! The people with initiative and drive were the ones who would succeed at Best Buy. That's still true today.

Even so, we couldn't have our buyers wandering around five warehouses with yellow pads, any more than you can have 251 store managers in twenty-nine states showing up at headquarters and asking for the key to the main warehouse.

Something had to be done.

MY RUSSIAN MOMENT

We decided—or, I should say, our IT people decided—that we needed outside help to do it. Early in 1996, we asked some of the major consultancies, including McKinsey & Company, PriceWaterhouse, and Andersen Consulting (the company that is now Accenture), to make proposals to us.

I will never forget Monday, March 11, 1996. That was the day we heard presentations from the consultants. I remember the Andersen presentation most vividly. The firm had two consultants there: a young man and the team leader, a woman in her midthirties. They both worked out of the Andersen office in Minneapolis. The project wasn't very big by consulting standards—$25,000 or so. But the consultants told me later that Andersen had been trying to get its foot in the door at Best Buy for years. One of the consultants used to drive by our headquarters every day on the way to work. He'd say to himself, *We really should be working with Best Buy. We could help them.* The fact that we didn't use consultants drove him crazy.

Andersen had invested considerable time and effort in the proposal for what the consultants called "retail simplification." They started by saying nice things about how Best Buy had been enormously successful over the years.

OK, we knew that, I thought.

They said that the kind of growth we were having now brought with it new challenges.

No kidding.

They told us that Andersen had extensive experience with helping retailers. I had to admit, the firm's credentials were impressive. It had worked with all the major retailers: Wal-Mart, Target, Sears, CVS, the Gap, Safeway.

Now that's impressive, I thought. *Maybe these guys know what they're talking about. They've actually done it for other companies— and big, successful ones at that!*

Then the consultants went through their "opportunity assessment." That was essentially code for "all the things you're doing wrong, which is pretty much everything, that we can help you fix." They said we had to get more efficient, handle deliveries better, make our pricing more consistent.

Got it.

Then came the part that made me see red and that ultimately won them the job: the secret shoppers. Andersen had sent people into Best Buy stores in twelve different markets around the country. Each shopper had a simple assignment: try to buy the item that had been featured in the Sunday advertising circular. It happened to be an Acer PC.

The results made my blood boil.

Only three of the twelve stores actually had the Acer computer in stock. I couldn't believe it. We were promoting a product in the newspaper that we didn't have in the store? How could this happen? Who was to blame?

It got worse. Not only was the item not in stock, but the salespeople had no idea *when* it would be in stock. And they had a solution: *Here, Ms. Secret Shopper, we will offer you this much nicer computer, which normally retails for two hundred dollars more than the one we advertised, at the same price!* Bye-bye, profit.

Some of the secret shoppers complained to the store managers. What did the store managers do? They said, *We're frustrated, too!*

Then came the last straw. One secret shopper had gone into a Best Buy store and asked for the Acer computer. The salesperson apologized; the product was not in stock. "But," he said, "I wouldn't advise you to buy it from us anyway. I'd suggest you go over to Circuit City and get it there." Ever helpful, he went so far as to draw the customer a map and give her directions.

I went ballistic. I took off my shoe and pounded the table with it. The consultants later called that my "Russian moment," evoking the time the notorious Russian premier Nikita Khrushchev allegedly did the same thing back in 1960 to express frustration during a meeting at the United Nations.

"This is totally and completely unacceptable!" I yelled. "I want to know which store it was. I want to know who the salesperson was! This cannot happen!"

They refused to give me names or locations. "That's not the point, Dick," they said. "It's not about the individuals. It's about the process." At last, I cooled down. I realized that what happens at the bottom of an organization is usually a reflection of what's going on at the top. This was no doubt a systemic problem and had to be addressed as such.

Anyway, Andersen got the business. Why? The consultants obviously had done their homework. They had gone into the stores, where the real action was. And they had done all this work on their own dime. I liked that.

The plan was for the project to be completed by September 1, 1996. The work took a little longer than that. In fact, fifteen years later, it's *still* going on. That's not a criticism. It's a recognition of the importance of continuous improvement.

THE MASTER PLAN

That summer, two important things happened.

First, working closely with Andersen, we came up with something called a Standard Operating Platform (SOP) for Best Buy. It was a comprehensive set of uniform practices and procedures for operating the stores that would accommodate fast growth and high employee turnover. It covered everything: How to staff a store. How to define the roles and responsibilities of each person. How to get a store ready to open in the morning. How to receive a shipment, unload a truck, and manage stock. How to display merchandise on the shelves. When to make price changes. How to interact with customers on the floor. How to answer the phones. How to manage cash. The whole enchilada. The SOP would provide the process to manage future growth and change in an orderly and consistent manner.

We tested the SOP in our Northtown, Minnesota, store. After some refinements and tweaks, we rolled it out to eight more stores and so on through the system. Through that process, we learned how to better achieve *change implementation*. It seems pretty obvious now, but it didn't then. We had undergone plenty of change in our history, and I had become very accustomed to it. But that change had been mostly about growth: We opened new stores and added new people. We got bigger. The *way* we did things, the processes and practices, hadn't changed much at all. Nor had the way we *thought* about the things we did. That was necessary now. To change how people think and behave takes a whole different set of skills than the ones you need to manage growth. That was the real work of the SOP project.

Let me give you just one example of how the SOP work played out. I'll start with an issue that I haven't talked much about: shrink. That is, loss of product due to theft. This is a chronic problem for any retailer and had always been a concern for Best Buy. As we got bigger, however, and our systems got more and more overburdened, the problem of shrink got even worse.

To give you an idea of just how bad it was, and what we did to overcome it during the SOP days, I'll let Paul Stone—who is now VP of Asset Protection and Risk Management—tell the story.

"My story begins on March 23, 1995. I was a member of a loss prevention leadership team and, on that day, we were scheduled for a budget review with the executive officers of the company. Just before the meeting started, we learned that our shrinkage expense was approximately twice what it had been just six months earlier. It had climbed to over one percent of sales revenue for the first time ever.

We presented this result to the executives and, needless to say, it did not go over well. We had a very difficult time explaining the situation. We started blaming everyone and everything. It was the fault of marketing, retail leadership, operations, inventory control systems, store systems. We blamed everyone but ourselves.

The executives did not buy it. They did everything they could to make us see that our department had become a silo. You don't reach out for help, the executives said. You don't create good internal partnerships. You're out of touch with the business. At the end of the very long day, the executives told us we had one year to fix the problem or we would be out.

We spent the next six months trying to improve our shrinkage expense outcomes. We didn't get very far, largely because we still couldn't develop strong partnerships with other internal leaders.

Finally, we went to see Brad Anderson, who was the president at the time, and asked for help. Brad said, 'What took you so long?' He called his leaders together. Shrinkage became everyone's *problem, not just a concern for the loss prevention team.*

Over the next six months, during which time the SOP was taking shape, we did a number of things that put us on the path to creating a low shrinkage culture. We held employee roundtables and asked people for their ideas about how to correct the shrinkage problem. Based on these ideas, we developed a company-wide shrinkage reduction plan and implemented it in every store. (It's essentially the same process we use today.) We held leaders accountable for executing the plan. We recognized and rewarded people for their achievements on the shrinkage issue. And we had some fun by creating a mascot called Shrink Stomper who helped us communicate how we were doing.

The shrinkage plan became part of the SOP. For the loss prevention team, the experience helped us understand the importance of change management, of becoming a learning organization, and of building internal partnerships. It certainly shaped my career and the careers of many others at Best Buy. We still talk about that story and the learnings that came from it."

While they were developing the SOP project, and as we began to have successes like the one we had with loss prevention, the Andersen consultants did what consultants do: they looked inside every closet and under every rock at Best Buy. They were amazed, shocked, and alarmed by what they found. It was clear that our problems were not confined to our stores. We had significant problems at headquarters, too. Purchasing . . . advertising . . . inventory management . . . computer systems . . . management structure—I mean *everything*. It seemed that the entire organization was one giant mess. Again, this was not surprising given how fast we had grown and the gaps in the skills of our management team (including me), but it was a mess all the same. We had been so consumed by building the business, we hadn't thought hard enough about systems and controls. Now we needed an organizational overhaul.

In October 1996, Andersen got the go-ahead to create a master plan for us. It would tackle some of the biggest issues, including product sourcing, the supply chain, forecasting, product assortment, and advertising. The result was a monster document that laid out a program called Process to Profits. It was a three-inch binder with four hundred pages of analysis and recommendations.

The Andersen people talked it through with Wade and Brad, but I was not yet in the loop. The plan was obviously far-reaching. The goal was to reengineer our processes and substantially increase our bottom line. It could have huge, positive results for our company. It would also cost a lot of money to implement.

"How much is a lot of money?" Wade asked the consultants. "Just for budgeting purposes."

"Forty-four million dollars," they replied.

"Forty-four million?" he asked. "You're kidding." He had earmarked $2 million in his budget. This would have to be discussed by the entire executive team, including me. Probably it would require a vote of the board to move forward.

I'm not sure we would have accepted the plan, except for one thing: that year we made almost no profit. It's not that our revenue wasn't growing. In fiscal year 1997, the twelve months from March 3, 1996, through March 1, 1997, we took in $7.758 billion. Almost *$8 billion*. But we made a profit of only *$1.7 million*. That was pathetic. It amounted to a profit of less than one-tenth of 1 percent. Outrageous! We had income of $46 million the previous year and $52 million the year before that. Our earnings per share had dipped to a negative number for the first time in our history.

All hell broke loose. Our share price dropped. Shareholders were questioning my leadership. Sandy wondered if I shouldn't ease myself out of the business. Not only did the performance results rock the company, but they got to people personally. I watched as my personal portfolio plunged in value. Employees throughout the company, almost all of whom owned Best Buy stock, could see their futures dimming. How would they afford to buy a house? How would they send their kids to college? What about their travel plans? What about retirement?

We had to do something, and we had to do it fast.

THE MILLION-DOLLAR OFFER EVERYBODY REFUSED

In March 1997, the senior team got together to talk about how to deal with the situation.

I knew that the SOP program was having some success. I did not yet know about the master plan.

I said, "Look, we've obviously still got an issue with inventory management. We've learned that we've got to find ways to accelerate and increase the turnover in our computer products. We're operating much too manually. We need to get into a higher level of rhythm and accuracy in fulfillment. We need to improve our communication with suppliers. I'm confident we can figure this out."

I looked around the table at Brad, Al, Wade, and Phil. They were nodding. But I could tell they were not believing what they were hearing. None of them had ever done anything like this before. They were being asked to take us to a whole new level of complexity. Could they handle it?

I looked at Brad and said, "Brad, I'd like you to take this on."

Brad had a blank look in his eyes. He said nothing, but I could tell what he meant: *I love ya, Dick, but I don't want to be set up for failure, because I don't have a clue about this.*

I turned to Wade. "Wade, I'm sure this is something that you, in your infinite wisdom, can get your hands around."

Wade rolled his eyes. "Well, I'm sure I could get it done, but I'm not convinced I can do it as quickly as we need it done."

I paused. I looked at each person in the room, one by one. "OK. What if I put a million dollars on the table for the person who takes this on? You can devote one hundred percent of your time and efforts to it. If you get results, I will personally write you a check for a million."

The room went quiet. There was shifting in the chairs. Clearing of throats. Eyes darted back and forth.

"Wade?" I thought for sure he would rise to the challenge.

Wade hemmed and hawed for a moment. Finally he said, "Dick, look. Nobody in this room is going to take that check, because it's the wrong answer. We can't do this ourselves. We have to get help from the outside."

Wow. I had just offered a $1 million bonus, with no strings attached, and everybody had turned it down. This was serious.

Wade took the opportunity to plunk the master plan on the table. He had been designated to introduce it to me and the rest of the group. He summarized the program. He highlighted the upside. Andersen predicted we could increase our profits from $2 million to $221 million within three years. We could realize billions in savings. It sounded way too good to be true. If Andersen had said we could double or even triple our earnings, maybe I would've believed it. But a hundredfold increase?

Finally, I asked the key question. "What's all this going to cost?"

Wade hesitated for a moment, then let the number fly. "Forty-four million dollars."

I genuinely could not believe what I was hearing. "Forty-four million dollars? Nobody pays forty-four million to anybody for anything!"

"Plus, they want a piece of the incremental savings," Wade added.

198 / BECOMING THE BEST

I felt like I wanted to jump out the window. "You guys have got to be kidding me."

"Not kidding. Forty-four million."

I don't remember much about the meeting after that.

I GIVE IN, MORE OR LESS

Over the next couple of days, I read the master plan. Every page of it. Carefully. In detail. It wasn't pretty. It was all I could do to get through it.

Brad came to see me. He had read through the report, too. "What do you think?" he asked.

"It's a pretty scathing indictment," I said. "It basically says that if we don't improve operations dramatically, we're doomed."

"Yes, it does," Brad said.

"But," I said, "I think they may be right."

I'm not sure what Brad's look signified. Chagrin? Embarrassment? Pain? He was president and chief operating officer. The report was saying that all the stuff Brad was responsible for was a mess.

"Dick," he said, "I think you should fire me."

I considered it—briefly. But I might as well have fired myself. Brad had always put Best Buy and its employees ahead of himself. It was largely because of that attitude (and a lot of other great qualities) that Brad was eventually named my successor as CEO and that he landed on the cover of the issue of *Fortune* magazine that named Best Buy as the best-managed company in America. Needless to say, I did not accept Brad's offer.

Three days later I called one of the consultants and asked him to come over. I had yet to talk directly with him, and I wanted to get the story straight from the horse's mouth.

It was just the two of us. We talked about our families a little bit.

I told him that my daughter Susan worked for the company and had recently been promoted to vice president.

Then we started going through the binder. The consultant told me later that he was surprised that I had read it all. Many of Andersen's clients would just read the executive summary. That came as a shock to me. This was a make-or-break decision for us. We had to be sure we were taking the right course of action and working with the right consultants. We couldn't invest $44 million and not get extraordinary results and value. I had to know all the details. So, not only had I read every word of the document, I then proceeded to ask a lot of questions.

I started with the hefty line item for a new computer system. "I really don't understand this," I said. "Every time the IT guys come in here, they want more money. I just don't see what I get for it. If we're going to spend this kind of money on a new system, I'm going to hold Andersen accountable. The new system has to make things better. You have to educate us about what our IT spending should be—how we can tell whether we're getting the bang for the buck that we should."

The consultant said, "Well, considering what you're spending on IT right now, Dick, I'm amazed that you get any product out the door at all. I honestly don't know how your people get it done. You ought to give them a medal."

That's what they had always told me!

"Really?" I asked.

"Really!"

"But here's what gets me," I said. "I still don't see why we can't handle this ourselves. Throughout our history, if we had a problem, I'd get the management team together on a Saturday morning. We could always figure it out. Why shouldn't we do that now?"

The consultant said, "Dick, listen, it's not a small company anymore. Best Buy is too big. You just can't operate that way anymore."

"Why can't we?"

The Andersen guy looked at me. "Listen, Dick, I've been running around Best Buy for the last few months."

"Yes?"

"I don't see you out and about a whole lot. When was the last time you walked out of this office and visited the managers who run supply chain or IT? Your managers. The people who run the regions and the districts. I know you visit stores. I'm not talking about the stores."

I tried to think: when had I last visited an office of one of my staff managers? I couldn't come up with anything. The managers always came to me.

"You just told me about your daughter's promotion," the consultant said. "How long ago was that?"

"About a year ago."

"And how many times have you visited her office in that year?"

Ouch. I had *never* been to Susan's office.

"You've never been to your own daughter's office? But you want to know why the rest of the company is not meeting around the breakfast table? You're just too big, Dick. You can't run this company like it's still at three hundred million."

That was a defining moment for me. Was I really an entrepreneur at heart? Or could I make the adjustment to leading a multibillion-dollar company? Unlike many entrepreneurs who make their exit when the company reaches a certain size, I felt I had much more to contribute to my company and the people who invested their careers in Best Buy. I decided that if Andersen could help us, I'd try to make the partnership work.

But I was still having a very hard time getting my head around the price tag. After meeting with the consultant, I had one final conversation with Brad, behind closed doors. Not only was the cost too high, I just couldn't believe we could get the kind of results

Andersen was promising. What if we spent the $44 million and didn't improve our profits at all?

Finally, Brad put it all on the line.

"Dick," he said, "there is no way you and I can solve this without help. In fact, it's what *we* haven't done that has gotten us into this situation. We're not the ones who can bring in the solution this time."

I hesitated. "Well . . ."

"So either we get on board with this . . . ," Brad said, and he paused. "Or I just can't do my job."

I could see that Brad was totally serious. Was he saying he would have to leave the company? If so, I had a choice to make. I could keep Brad on, but I would have to pony up the $44 million to pay the consultants. Alternatively, I could not spend the money and . . . do what? Lose Brad? And maybe others, too? After all, every executive on my team had turned down the $1 million bonus. What was I going to do—go down to the warehouse myself and spend my days tracking inventory with a yellow pad?

I made up my mind—reluctantly. I recommended to the board that we move forward on Andersen's proposal, and the directors approved.

Was I completely, utterly convinced it would work? No.

Did I really want to bring in Andersen and pay the firm $44 million plus a percentage of our gains? No—the very thought of it was painful.

Did we bring the consultants in anyway? Yes. Why? Well, perhaps the deciding factor was Andersen's experience with Wal-Mart. As one of our directors pointed out, much of Wal-Mart's success was based on the company's ability to manage information in order to make its supply chain one of the most effective in the world. What Andersen had learned by working with Wal-Mart would certainly be applicable to Best Buy.

What's more, I wanted to make a smart management decision, rather than be influenced by my personal view of outsiders. I remembered how I had felt when I worked at the Red Owl grocery store. I didn't want to be like the store manager there, who wouldn't listen to my good ideas about how to stock the shelves. I realized that Andersen was essentially making a good suggestion. There was a risk in taking the advice, but I decided there was greater danger in not doing so.

Soon enough, Andersen was hard at work—with a team of fifty people! The firm's commitment and enthusiasm for the work made the price tag a little easier for me to deal with. Just a little.

THE SUMMIT

But that didn't mean *I* had to be personally involved. My plan was to stay on the sidelines. Andersen had to prove the plan was going to work. This wasn't my baby. I wanted them to own it.

What I didn't understand at the time was that consultants can be effective only if they have a true partnership with the leadership team. The CEO cannot sit back and be an observer. Fortunately, Andersen understood how important it was for me to get involved.

One day the team leader from Andersen more or less barged into my office. "Dick, look, people need to learn what this is all about," she said. "They're going to have to change the way they do their jobs. They will have to make decisions that are very different from the ones they're used to making."

"Yes?"

"Process to Profits involves major change. People will posture. They'll dig in their heels. They'll try to sabotage it."

"How do you suggest we prevent that?"

"Dick, we need *you*. We need your sponsorship and your leadership. People have to know that you support this. That you believe in it. Remember, you just signed up for a forty-four–million-dollar contract—and that's just a start as the results begin to show."

The problem was that I didn't fully believe in the program. Yet. "What do you want me to do?" I asked.

"We want you to hold a summit meeting of your top leaders. All fifty of them. A full-day event," she said. "And you'll be the main speaker."

She could tell that she had some convincing to do.

"Can I show you something?" she asked.

She popped a DVD into the player. She pressed play. It was a scene from the movie *Apollo 13*. It featured Tom Hanks playing Jim Lovell, the mission commander. He and his crew are in outer space and running out of oxygen fast. A team of engineers is on the ground. They have never worked together before. They have to figure out a fix for the problem, using only the odds and ends the astronauts have in the spacecraft. There is no time to waste.

"Why on earth are you showing me this?" I asked.

"Because this is what we're asking people at Best Buy to do, Dick," she said. "They have to work together to figure out solutions to very difficult problems, using only what they have at hand."

OK, so retail is not rocket science. But I did see parallels between our situation and the Apollo 13 mission.

The team leader jumped to another scene. This one featured Gene Kranz, the flight director, played by actor Ed Harris. The spacecraft is running low on electrical power. If the astronauts don't conserve what they have, they won't have enough juice to fire their rockets upon reentry. The engineers have to figure out a way to keep the spacecraft running on a trickle. Here's what Kranz says to them:

> *I want you guys to find every engineer who designed every switch, every circuit, every transistor, and every light bulb that's up there. Then I want you to talk to the guy on the*

assembly line who actually built the thing. Find out how to squeeze every amp out of both of these goddamned machines. We never lost an American in space; we're sure as hell not gonna lose one on my watch. Failure is not an option!"

That scene really got to me. It was about the importance of leadership. The Andersen people were showing me the kind of role I could play, the kind of role I *had* to play, to make this all work. From that moment, I was on board—every bit as much as Tom Hanks was on board that spacecraft.

It was a compelling reminder of the importance of leadership. Of course, failure had not been an option when we opened our first Sound of Music store and mortgaged our home . . . when we created the first Best Buy store . . . when we took on Highland . . . when we introduced Concept II . . . when we had to improvise inventory in new Chicago stores.

Andersen was clarifying the kind of role I had to play—even when a massive consulting team was engaged—so we could take on Circuit City in the national market. I totally got it. We could outsource for expertise when needed, but there was no way we could outsource leadership. It was a great lesson on partnering with consultants to bring about change. Brad had convinced me we couldn't get the job done without consultants—but the Andersen people convinced me they couldn't get it done without us as well.

Next, our marketing staff said we needed a theme for the summit meeting. We decided to steal our theme—*Failure Is Not an Option*—from the line in the movie. It was a little strange, because we had always said that it was OK to make mistakes—after all, that's how you learn. But in 1997, we had made more than our share of them. Now we needed a big win.

The summit was a success. I spoke as passionately as I could about the project. Those who know me well say I make up for any other deficiency I may have (at least partially) with the abundance of passion that comes through when I speak in public about something I feel strongly about.

After I spoke, I asked each manager to come up to the stage individually and make a pledge to support the mission. We made up special posters, and I signed one for everybody who attended the meeting.

As part of the summit, we did a little exercise. We asked everyone to imagine a headline for a newspaper article they would like to see in the future. We read some of them aloud. One read, *Best Buy Honored As One of the Most Respected Companies for Its Amazing Turnaround and Greatest Stock Growth.*

Everybody in the audience laughed. It sounded too outrageous.

Two years later, an article about Best Buy in the *Washington Post* ran with the headline *The Fastest Turnaround in Retail History.* The moral of the story: any ambitious, company-wide initiative needs full buy-in from all hands—starting with those at the top and encompassing everyone in the organization.

A MODEST EXPENSE?

In the end, we didn't pay Andersen $44 million. With the 10 percent gain-sharing on the $1.3 billion savings they helped us achieve, we paid the firm more like $105 million. I didn't mind, because the results were astounding. (Well, I didn't mind *too* much.) After all, we got what was promised and much, much more.

What did we do during that period? A better question would be *What didn't we do?* It would take another whole book to describe the program. We revamped almost every one of our processes. We

The Process to Profits program required all hands on deck.

got better and smarter at purchasing, shipping, merchandising, sourcing, advertising, and managing our product portfolio. We basically reinvented the whole back end of our company. We went from "not so good" to "best in class."

And it's important to say that the Process to Profits program was a company-wide effort. Everybody got involved. Failure was not an option. Neither was disengagement.

Let me give you just a few examples of what we accomplished together over a three-year period.

Remember the secret shopper problem? The out-of-stock Acer computer? My Russian moment? My first reaction had been to look to the salesperson or the store manager. Of course, they were not really at fault. The issue was much deeper and more complicated. And it was not *just* about out-of-stocks.

The problem was that we didn't really have a defined process for choosing which merchandise to buy, which products to feature in our advertising, and how to determine the best assortment for each store. Our internal buyers in the home office (known as "merchants") did the buying. They didn't have enough information about which products were moving in which stores. And they sometimes purchased items that looked like good deals, but that we couldn't sell at a profit.

We discovered that, in general, we were stocking too many items. Remember, we believed in giving the customer control. And we had equated control with lots of choice and a full assortment of products. So we might stock twenty different TVs in a particular category. But something funny happens when there is too *much* choice. The customer feels confused and *out* of control. Then the customer says, "I have to go home and think about it." We were setting ourselves up to lose a sale.

What's more, we were making a profit on only six or seven of those twenty TVs. We actually lost money on some of them. As the consultants said about one model, "Every time you sell one of these TVs, you're paying the customer five bucks to take it off your hands!"

So, we trimmed our product assortment, tightened up our purchasing procedures, and got much more disciplined about which products we featured in our advertising. The Sunday newspaper insert has always been the mainstay of our advertising. Getting space in the ad had been a battle between merchants. Whoever exerted the most pressure and fought the hardest got the space they wanted. We changed all that. We advertised the items that we had in stock, that we knew would sell, that the customers wanted, and that would deliver a profit to us. What a concept!

But it wasn't all about cost cutting and process improvement. We also came up with some marketing and promotional innovations. One of the most successful of these was the "doorbuster."

The holiday retailing season begins on the day after Thanksgiving, which is known in retail as Black Friday. It's called that because it's

The doorbuster—a Best Buy invention.

considered the first day of the year that retailers actually start to earn a profit, or "go into the black." The rest of the year we take in enough to keep the lights on and pay our people. The holiday period is when we make most of our profit.

Well, we studied what actually happens on Black Friday. We found that the largest volume of shoppers came to our stores between noon and 5:00 P.M. The stores got so crowded that we could barely handle the traffic. People got frustrated. They didn't want to wait in line. They would buy less—or leave without buying anything.

How could we even out the traffic flow? We decided to open our doors earlier than usual, at 7:00 A.M. rather than 8:00 A.M. The first two hundred people who showed up would receive a special deal: a PC at half price.

Wow. On Black Friday morning of 1997, we started getting calls from managers at 6:00 A.M.: "I've got people lining up all the way down the street!" We found that those early birds bought the computer *and* they did most of the rest of their holiday shopping at Best Buy. The results were phenomenal. We just blew the doors off, and it was an amazing kickoff to the holiday season.

Today, most retailers run doorbuster campaigns. The openings get earlier and earlier each year, and the deals get crazier and crazier. You have Best Buy to thank for this Black Friday madness!

We rebounded incredibly fast. Holiday season 1996 was the year of the computer debacle. After holiday season 1997, one trade publication named Best Buy as the year's highest-performing retailer.

Wall Street took careful notice of what was going on at Best Buy. In August, Salomon Brothers recommended purchase of our stock.

In October, a report from the investment firm DLJ read, "Best Buy is in the midst of creating best practices in many of its operations. This two-year plan is just beginning to yield benefits."

In December, Merrill Lynch said, "The recovery in Best Buy's profitability has been sharp and much better than we anticipated."

In March 1998, we were really in favor. A report from ABN AMRO said, "To be sure, Best Buy's U-turn has been nothing short of spectacular. Management's focus on a more profitable product mix improving inventory productivity and the effectiveness of its advertising program . . . has delivered dramatic top- and bottom-line results in a short period of time."

Our share price started to climb and kept on climbing. It went from a low of $2 per share in March 1997 to a high of about $46 per share at the end of February 1999. As a result, our market capitalization—the total value of the company—soared from $403 million to more than $9 billion from fiscal year 1997 through fiscal year 1999. That's an increase of 2,192 percent.

And that profit figure? Andersen hit the mark. From $1.7 million profit in 1997, we went to $94.5 million in 1998 and a record $224.4

million for fiscal year 1999. Andersen had predicted an increase to $221 million. Not bad.

I gave (and still give) Andersen a tremendous amount of credit for the firm's role in the turnaround. I even started downplaying the cost. I was quoted in the *Washington Post* as saying, "It was a relatively modest expense, but it allowed us to . . . come up with a game plan that we have gotten wonderful benefit from, without a tremendous amount of infighting."

Talk about a turnaround!

As much credit as I give to Andersen, I also have to say that people throughout the Best Buy organization—from the folks at headquarters to people in the warehouse network and in the stores—made the turnaround happen. Our people rolled up their sleeves and contributed huge amounts of creativity, innovation, and sheer hard work to the effort. Andersen was a partner but hardly the only player. It's not as if the consultants told us what to do, and we simply executed. We really did create a strong partnership and it paid off in a big way.

Once it became clear that we were out of the woods, I thought I could afford to ease up a bit. I had pledged to Sandy that I would devote two years to the turnaround and then I would consider pulling back from active management. She and I had always agreed that, after our three decades of hard work together building Best Buy, we could look forward to much more time together in our later years.

Unfortunately, it didn't turn out that way.

A COMPANY
IS A FAMILY

MY NAME IS ON THE COVER OF THIS BOOK, BUT I HAVE to give my late wife, Sandy, credit as coauthor of the Best Buy story. She didn't have a formal title or a position in the company hierarchy. She didn't attend board meetings. She didn't vote on stock offerings. She didn't hire or fire anybody. But I could not have built Best Buy without her. She was my best consultant and most trusted adviser. She helped keep me on track. She allowed me to work as hard as I needed to, when I needed to. She didn't complain when my days stretched to twelve hours. She didn't moan when I had to travel out of town.

I don't want to give the impression that Sandy was only a behind-the-scenes supporter. That would not be accurate. She was an active participant in the life of the company. In the early days, our dinner table often doubled as a conference table. Sandy strongly believed in the value of breaking bread with others. She thought it was important to sit down, have a meal, and really get to know the other person.

Sandy's involvement went well beyond breakfast, lunch, or dinner. If we needed an extra pair of hands at the cash register, Sandy was there. At new store openings, she would set up the big coffee urns and arrange the food. She helped lay out the Sunday ads. Later, whenever she could, she traveled with me wherever I had to go. She knew people throughout the company, she talked to everybody, and she helped anyone who needed help.

Sandy only asked for one thing. She wanted me to assure her that I would someday step back from the company, at least a little, and we would have time to spend together traveling, visiting kids and grandkids, and doing charitable work. I made that pledge, but it was a promise I was unable to keep—not because I didn't want to, and not because I didn't try. It was because, as I discovered, I could not completely control my destiny, or hers.

The only consolation I can take in Sandy's passing is the way my family, colleagues, and friends at the company responded to her illness and death. During this very difficult time in my life, they showed me that a company really is a family—a very large, diverse, and complicated family, but a family nonetheless.

I tell Sandy's story in this chapter, not only as a memorial to her, but also as a way to remind us of the importance of the human side of our company. We're a business organization, for sure, but we're also a group of people. We have to be mindful that we all have our troubles and go through hard times, just as I did. It's our responsibility to help one another as much as we can, whenever we can.

I certainly came through this dark period in my life with a deepened appreciation of family and relationships. In particular, I thought a lot about how important it is to find a good balance between life at work and life outside of work.

I also renewed my belief in the importance of giving back to the community. Best Buy had been involved in philanthropy for many years before Sandy died, but in the years following her passing we really stepped up our charitable activities. I am very proud to say that philanthropic work has become a way of life for Best Buy. It is also a key focus for me personally.

I think of our charitable work as just one of Sandy's many legacies.

DON'T FORGET THE GUYS IN CAR AUDIO

Above all, Sandy cared about people. When the company was small, Sandy would show her concern just as my mother had done. If somebody was sick, she'd make a meal and deliver it to the house. If you needed to talk about how you were doing, she was available for a conversation and counsel.

As the company grew, Sandy made sure that we still paid close attention to Best Buy people. One way to do that was to make regular store visits, and the two of us would often go together. I have always scheduled my days as fully as possible. I like to start with a meeting at 7:30 A.M. and keep going through the dinner hour, ending the day around 7:00 P.M. When visiting stores outside the Twin Cities,

Sandy and I breaking bread together.

I would usually schedule at least three stops a day, sometimes four. That meant we had to keep moving.

I remember one visit distinctly. Sandy and I flew in early that morning. The store manager greeted us, introduced us to three or four of his people, and whisked us off on a tour. They showed us new displays, talked about sales outcomes, and described some programs they were developing. They showed us around the floor and escorted us through the warehouse.

At certain stops along the way, Sandy would deliberately engage the managers in conversation, so I could spend a few minutes with the folks in each department. She would ask the managers about their families, their vacation plans, what kinds of foods they liked best. Meanwhile, I could talk to the people who do the everyday work of the company—the blue shirts in sales, the yellow shirts in security, the black or white shirts who handle service. While Sandy chatted with the managers, I got the details about what was going on in every department. This is how store visits typically went, and I learned things during those tours that I might not have been told otherwise.

Our tour was about over, and I had my eye on the clock because we had to get moving to the next store. I finished up with the folks in the appliance department, and I headed for the front door.

"Wait a minute," Sandy said. "Did you talk to the people in car audio?"

"No," I said, checking my watch. "We don't really have time."

"Dick, we're not leaving until you sit down and talk with the car audio installers."

"Honey, we've got another store to visit. I promise you I'll talk with the installers at the next store."

"No, Dick," she said. "These guys knew you were coming. They've been waiting to see you. If you ignore them, they'll never forget it. You have to speak with them."

What could I say? "OK, honey. Let's go."

Sandy marched me back to the car audio area. Just as she said, two installers and the department supervisor were waiting patiently to talk with me. They gave me big smiles and hearty handshakes. We got right down to it, going over every aspect of their operation. What product lines were they thinking of adding? Was their install rate what it should be? Were they working the right number of hours? Did they have enough space to do the job right? Thirty minutes later, we were out the door.

Sandy was dogged during those visits. I could not leave a store without touching every department. She took every chance she could to make contact as well. On one occasion, we walked past a young woman who was vacuuming the carpet. The woman was very pregnant and obviously feeling it. Sandy stopped and gently took the woman by the arm.

"I think you need a little break," she said. "Why don't you sit down for a few minutes?" Sandy guided the woman to a chair and then grabbed the vacuum herself. "I'll take care of this." And she finished vacuuming the floor.

That was Sandy.

THE WORST SIX MONTHS OF MY LIFE

Sandy loved the holidays, but in the weeks before Christmas 2000, she wasn't enjoying the season as she usually did. She went out shopping and came home feeling tired. She walked up the stairs and was out of breath before she reached the second floor. We figured she was coming down with something—maybe the flu or even pneumonia. We didn't know.

On Christmas Eve the whole family gathered at the house as we always did—all four of our kids and the five grandchildren we had at the time. We were looking forward to an evening together—opening presents and sharing a meal. Sandy felt weak, though, and had no energy. She didn't want to expose any of the young people, so she stayed at the top of the stairs, leaning on the railing, watching as we opened our gifts, smiling and chiming in as much as she could. The evening ended a little earlier than usual.

The next day, the kids celebrated Christmas at their own homes. Sandy and I were alone. She felt so exhausted, she spent the whole day in bed. The following morning she still wasn't feeling any better, so I called our family doctor. He was able to squeeze us in that afternoon. I drove Sandy to his office, and he took an X-ray of her chest. He studied the picture carefully.

"I've never seen anything like this before," he said at last. "One lung is clear and looks perfectly fine. But the other lung . . ." He looked even more closely at the film. "The other lung is completely white. It seems to be filled with fluid. I really don't know what it is. I think you should see a pulmonary specialist."

The doctor called United Hospital and arranged for Sandy to meet with a specialist. We drove there immediately and checked her in, and they started running tests that very day. One test led to another. The pulmonologist consulted with a pathologist and other specialists. The process continued for two full days. I stayed with Sandy as much as I could, dashing back and forth to the office for meetings. I wasn't there when the doctor came into Sandy's room to discuss the test results.

"Sandy," he said, "I need to talk with you and your husband." She called me, and I drove to the hospital right away.

"Do you remember Steve McQueen, the movie star?" the doctor asked us.

I remembered his movies, of course, and vaguely recalled that he had died in Mexico, where he had gone seeking treatment for cancer.

"McQueen had a very rare type of cancer. It's called meso-thelioma. It's caused by exposure to asbestos. Sandy has the same thing."

We looked at him in disbelief.

"Unfortunately, this is a cancer that's not easily controlled," the doctor said. "In fact, the success rate in treating it is less than one-tenth of 1 percent. I'm sorry to say that the life expectancy is six months to two years."

We could not comprehend what we were hearing.

We listened in shock as the doctor described the cancer to us in detail. We learned that it is caused by exposure to asbestos at a time much earlier in the person's life. The asbestos fibers can lie dormant in the body for thirty, forty, or fifty years with absolutely no ill effects. But then, in a small number of people, a cancerous tumor begins to grow. It develops in the pleural lining, which is the protective lining around the lungs. When the body detects the cancer, it fights back by creating a protective fluid. This collects between the lining of the lung and the lung itself. Eventually, the fluid puts so much pressure on the lung that it collapses and can barely take in any air. The fluid is what showed up white on Sandy's X-ray. It was making her tired and short of breath. It was killing her.

The doctor left us alone, and Sandy crumpled up. "Well, that's it," she said. "My life is over."

I was not going to give up. "No way," I said. "We can fight this. I'll get hold of the Mayo Clinic. We'll find a way."

I took Sandy home, then called Brad and said that I would not be coming in to the office for a while. Sandy was sick, and I had to stay with her. True to form, Brad stepped right up. He was chief operating officer, so he was already looking after day-to-day operations. He and Al could fill in for me when needed.

A few days later, Sandy checked in to the Mayo Clinic. We met with a team of doctors, who ran more tests. They confirmed the diagnosis of mesothelioma.

Our primary care doctor said, "The good news is that the cancer is stage one. It's local, confined to one lung. But it's going to require very aggressive treatment because it's a very aggressive cancer."

The doctors outlined a plan for treatment. First, they would do chemotherapy to shrink the tumor as much as possible. They would then surgically remove the affected lung and the lining around it. They would also take the lining from around the heart and replace the diaphragm with Gore-Tex to prevent the cancer from spreading to those areas. They would replace the natural linings with a synthetic Teflon material. The procedure would be long and involved, but it was Sandy's best and possibly only chance for survival. After she recovered from the surgery, she would undergo a course of radiation to finish off any remaining cancer cells.

It was obvious that Sandy would need full-time care and support. I announced to the company that Sandy was fighting a rare cancer called mesothelioma. We were learning as much about it as we could, and we were going to fight it as hard as we possibly could. I would not be at work until we had met this challenge. I said that, for now, I was passing the baton to Brad and Al. I trusted them completely to lead the company. I told them I would be at home and to call me if they really needed me.

And so began the most difficult six months of our lives together. The chemotherapy began, with treatments three weeks apart. Sandy was a real trooper throughout. However, she was convinced the treatments weren't working because, unlike most people who receive chemotherapy, she didn't lose any of her hair as part of the process.

What could have caused this cancer? We guessed that Sandy must have been exposed to asbestos early in our marriage. In 1963, before we had children, she worked in the Teachers Retirement department for the State of Minnesota. The office was in an old government building with exposed heating pipes that were probably wrapped with asbestos insulation. Fibers can easily break free and circulate through the ventilation system. No other explanation made sense to us.

After many weeks of chemo, the doctors decided that it was time for the surgery. The operation lasted nine hours. Sandy spent two days in intensive care, and then we went home.

When she felt a little better, we flew to Florida so she could get some sun and gather strength for the next round of treatments. She was very weak and could walk only a little. It took nearly three months before she felt she could endure the radiation. During that time, I tried to get her to exercise as much as possible. I'd help get her tennis shoes on and coax her to walk a little. I'd fix lunch and try to get her down to the kitchen to eat. But often she couldn't even manage that.

Finally, the doctors thought we should go ahead with the radiation. We flew back from Florida. Sandy checked in to the hospital. While they were determining exactly where and how much radiation she would need, the doctors noticed that fluid was collecting on her remaining lung.

"How often does this cancer traverse from one lung to the other?" I asked the doctor. "One lung is already gone. She only has two."

"It's quite unusual for that to happen," he said. "Probably in fifteen percent of cases. But with Sandy, we're pretty convinced that we got all the cancer during the surgery. The likelihood of it going to the other lung is slim."

Just to be sure, they took another X-ray along with a sample of the fluid in the second lung. The doctor said he would let us know the results as soon as possible.

The next day, I drove to the Ridgedale Mall to pick up something for Sandy—I forget exactly what it was. It was late May and raining cats and dogs. I dashed into the store, bought the item, and ran through the rain to the car. I noticed that I had a message waiting on my car phone. It was the doctor.

I called immediately. The doctor had very bad news. Not only had the cancer spread to the other lung, it was present around the heart, too.

I could not accept this. "So, what do we do next?" I asked. "There must be something else we can do."

"Dick," the doctor said, "I'm sorry, but we're not optimistic that anything we do will help."

"What about a transplant?" I asked. "Can't we do a lung transplant? Wouldn't that solve it?"

"No, we can't do a transplant," he said. "It's too late. She's too weak."

"What about drugs?" I asked. "There must be some other medicines we can try."

"Dick, we've given her the most effective treatments we have," he said. "Yes, there are other drugs, but they are likely to have even less success."

"There must be something else we can do," I said. "You mean, there's nothing else we can try? That's it?"

"Anything we do now will probably just weaken her," he said. "Whatever time she has is probably better spent without chemo or drugs or other interventions."

I realized that we had come to the end of the road. I said nothing for a few moments.

"Do you want me to tell Sandy?" the doctor asked at last.

"No," I said. "Thank you, Doctor, but Sandy and I have been in this together for the past six months. I can tell her."

People often say that I'm not very emotional. I can be reserved, a little formal. I cried only twice during the forty years that Sandy and I were married. The first time was when our beloved family dog died. He had lived with us for fourteen years. The second time was after the call with the doctor. I hung up and started to bawl. I sat in the car, the rain pouring down, and cried and cried and cried.

Finally, I gathered myself together. I drove slowly home. I told Sandy that the doctor had called. They had the test results. The cancer had moved to the other lung and the heart. The doctors said there was nothing more they could do. I asked her what she wanted. Should we try another round of chemo? Look for other drugs? Seek another opinion?

"No," she said. "There's no point. It is what it is."

She rapidly worsened. She didn't want to go to the hospital. She had oxygen to help her breathe. I redid the entertainment system so she could watch TV when she felt like it. Every day, I brought flowers in from the garden. The kids visited as often as they could, but it was very difficult for them to see their mother in this condition.

One Friday afternoon, Sandy's condition changed markedly. I was downstairs making dinner. Our daughter, Debra, was with me. She was thirty-two and had been a tremendous help to us both during the course of Sandy's illness. Suddenly, Sandy called for me. I hurried upstairs. She needed help to the bathroom. She seemed different than she had been just an hour before. I could tell she did not have long to live.

When I got her back to bed, I asked Debra to call the other children and tell them to come over immediately. She did and then joined me at Sandy's bedside. Ten minutes later Sandy died, with Debra and me holding her hands. All the kids were there within a half hour.

That following week we had the wake. We started at 4:00 P.M., and 2,700 people came to pay their respects. I shook the last hand at 11:00 P.M. We held Sandy's funeral mass at Nativity, the same church where we had been married back in June 1962. It is a beautiful, big church that holds at least eight hundred people, and it was jampacked.

Sandy's death was a defeat, a bitter defeat. We were so close to my finally slowing down at work. We were looking forward to twenty more years together, maybe more. We had bought a new house in Florida that we both loved. Sandy had a beautiful garden there. We wanted to travel the world.

Sandy was a special lady. She cared for everybody around her. Everybody loved her. But we had to deal with the cards we were dealt. There was no explaining it. It was the passage of life—a destiny, perhaps, and one outside of my control. Our faith puts our life in God's hands. We trust that He knows best, even though we don't always understand. To this day, I thank my children, Susan, Debra, Nancy, and Rick, for their support through this experience.

BACK AT THE RANCH

Ironically, while we were struggling with Sandy's illness, Best Buy was going through a period of incredibly robust health. Sales continued to climb. Profits soared. In 1999, we hit number twenty-five on the *BusinessWeek* 50 Best Performers list, *Fortune* named Best Buy as one of the top ten stocks of the decade, and I was personally honored by Ernst & Young as Entrepreneur of the Year.

We were opening stores like there was no tomorrow. In the year 2000 we opened forty-seven stores to bring the national total to 357 units in thirty-eight states. We entered the New York City market, perhaps the toughest place for retailers. I had been avoiding New York for years, because the costs there are so high and the risks so great. In September 2000, we had our grand opening, complete with a concert by Sting in Central Park. We gave away twenty thousand tickets.

Sandy and I at the New York Stock Exchange.

We were also pursuing a number of acquisitions to further fuel our growth and increase our strength in particular business areas. In 2000, we purchased a company called Magnolia Hi-Fi. The company dominated its segment of the business—high-end audio and video equipment in the Pacific Northwest. Magnolia was based in Seattle and had been doing business on the West Coast for more than fifty years. We saw acquisition of the chain as a way for us to get deeper into higher-income households and attract customers who wanted to buy premium products.

In December 2000, just a few weeks before Sandy became ill, we announced that we would make our largest purchase yet: the Musicland chain. The company operated relatively small stores, typically less than 5,000 square feet, in which it sold a very wide assortment of music and movie software. Also headquartered in the Twin Cities, Musicland had long been a thorn in our side, as the second-largest DVD retailer in the country (after us). Musicland was struggling financially—largely due to competition from us—and carried about $260 million in debt. But the stores had some very well-known brand names, including Sam Goody's, and operated 1,300 retail outlets.

Musicland was particularly strong in malls, where Best Buy did not have a presence. The plan was to transform the Musicland offering by adding a wide range of music-related and other digital products, including MP3 players, satellite systems, gaming systems, and accessories. We thought that Musicland would bring us lots of new mall customers, particularly women, as well as early adopters of technology, especially young ones.

The acquisition was not going to be a slam dunk, however, because of Musicland's rocky finances and the volatility of software retailing. Our board of directors had an intense debate about whether to buy the company. At $425 million in cash, plus the debt, it was an expensive acquisition for us. We decided to go ahead, and almost immediately we got into trouble. When news of the purchase was announced on December 7, our stock dropped by about 20 percent. This was not what we were hoping for.

In early 2001, we were also negotiating the acquisition of Future Shop, Canada's largest retailer of consumer electronics. We had

Our corporate campus in Richfield, Minnesota.

been looking at the Canadian market for a long time, because it is big and lucrative. By purchasing Future Shop, which operated eighty stores across Canada, we would be able to jump-start our business in Canada.

In addition to our acquisitions, we were getting ready to break ground for our new world headquarters campus—the 4.3-acre, 1.5-million-square-foot, $300 million, four-building complex just off Highway 494 in Richfield, where we are still headquartered today.

It was an incredibly exciting and hectic time for Best Buy, but I wasn't an active participant in all the activity from January 2001 through the end of June, when Sandy passed away. That summer, when I turned my attention to the company once again, I began to wonder whether I should permanently return as CEO. Brad was running the show. The company was doing well.

Besides, there was another factor, a new element to consider.

DIVINE PROVIDENCE

Early in Sandy's illness, I was talking to anybody and everybody about the disease. I wanted to learn as much as I could about treatments and outcomes. One day I got a call from a woman who worked in our travel department.

"Mr. Schulze, my sister's husband has the same form of cancer that your wife does," she said. "He was treated at Mayo Clinic and has been living with mesothelioma for two years now. I thought you might like to be in touch with my sister. Her name is Maureen Green."

I called the number. A woman with a very pleasant voice answered. I introduced myself and asked after her husband. She said that he was doing pretty well. In fact, he had even returned to work for a few hours each day. We immediately got into the details. Mrs. Green told me that her husband, Lowell, had worked for Goodyear for a short time after graduating from high school. One of his jobs was to install brake drums, which, at the time, had asbestos linings. Grinding them created a lot of dust and airborne particles, so it was clear where he had been exposed.

Mrs. Green asked about Sandy. I said that she was not doing very well, but that we were doing our best to be optimistic at this early stage in the process. We talked about the progression from chemo to surgery to radiation. She was very generous with her time. Our conversation gave Sandy and me a small ray of hope.

The next few months were, of course, a blur of hospital visits and tests and treatments. I didn't think much about Mrs. Green or her husband. I guess I assumed that, if he had gone back to work, he was probably on the road to recovery. Sadly, I later learned that Lowell had passed away at the end of April, during the time that Sandy was recovering from her surgery.

Six weeks later, Sandy died. At the wake, Elliot and his wife, Eloise, were standing in the long line, waiting to greet me and our family. They got to chatting with the woman behind them. She said that she had been in touch with me about her husband and that she had come to pay her respects. Her name was Maureen Green.

When Maureen introduced herself to me, I felt a tremendous connection with her. We hugged. We talked for a few moments. She seemed like someone very special. Eloise saw immediately that this relationship could grow into something important.

That summer, even as I was grieving for Sandy, I began to spend time sharing thoughts and emotions with Maureen. I found that her values were very much the same as Sandy's had been. She had six children and placed a tremendous focus on family, just as Sandy had. Maureen and I were both of the same faith. We had friends and neighbors in common. We enjoyed each other's company. We shared the bond of having lost a spouse.

I said to myself, *This just feels really right.* I found myself falling in love with Maureen. I guess you could call it Divine Providence.

Late in the summer, I spent some time at our lake cottage. Some of the kids and grandkids were there, keeping me company. My oldest grandson, Taylor—Susan's oldest child—wanted to be with me constantly. He was about ten at the time.

"Grandpa, can we go for a boat ride?" he'd ask. "Grandpa, can we go fishing?"

Despite my budding relationship with Maureen, I was still grieving and feeling kind of sorry for myself. I just couldn't respond to Taylor's needs. I kept telling him that I couldn't do anything at the moment—maybe later.

Then a strange thing happened. I heard Sandy's voice as if she were speaking directly to me.

"Dick," she said, "this is your grandson! He wants to be with you. He wants to do things with you. You're such a special grandpa." It was just what Sandy would have said if she were alive.

It woke me up. I said to myself, "Here I am." Taylor and I spent the rest of that weekend together, doing whatever he wanted to do.

I started to think even harder about what I wanted to do next. I was only sixty. I was young for retirement, but had been running the company since I was twenty-six—almost thirty-five years. I had never intended to stay on as CEO until I turned sixty-five, the usual retirement age. The company was doing well. It would be a very good time to make the transition to another leader. Besides, I had promised Sandy that I would step back from the business within a couple of years. If I didn't step back now, when would I?

I made up my mind that the time had come. I would step down as CEO. In September 2001, I revealed my intentions to the board. The directors understood. They asked me to stay on as chairman.

"I'm not leaving," I said. Once I had assured them I wasn't going anywhere, only one question remained: *Who would my successor be?*

BRAD OR WADE?

The rumors and wondering started to circulate: *Dick is stepping down! Who will take over? Will it be Brad? He is chief operating officer and vice chairman, after all. What about Wade? He's president of strategic business development. Which one will it be? Or maybe they'll bring in someone from the outside?*

It was not a simple decision. There was no question that Wade Fenn was incredibly capable. He had been with the company for almost twenty-two years. He had been through the battles and the growth with us. He knew the business inside and out. He was a big thinker and strong idea person.

And Brad? Brad didn't have the same talents that Wade had. He probably wasn't as aggressive in some ways. But Brad had other, equally impressive qualities. He was honest, trustworthy, focused, totally dependable, and passionate about working as hard as he could

Brad and Janet Anderson.

to get done what needed to be accomplished. He had started with us in 1973, when we were still Sound of Music, almost thirty years earlier. He had built an incredible network of friends and colleagues both within the company and outside the company. He was trusted by many and yet incredibly humble; he always gave others credit for successes. There was no question that Brad had given the company his all. Brad was the guy who had suffered through the CES show in Las Vegas. He had won over Ron Graham, the Better Business Bureau chief. He had lived in a Motel 6 for weeks during the battle to defeat Highland Superstores. During Sandy's illness, he had been like a rock, both for me and for the company.

Brad and I are incredibly different people. Brad is an abstract thinker; I am more pragmatic. Brad is a pessimist; I'm an optimist. Where I see opportunity, Brad sees disaster waiting to happen. Brad and I have often disagreed about how best to handle a situation. We argue often, even sometimes when we appear to be in violent agreement.

Brad was a quintessential member of the Best Buy *family*. He didn't have to talk about the values—he embodied them. He lived them every day. I knew he would always do whatever it took to help the company succeed. He would never, ever do anything that would put the company in harm's way. He cared tremendously about the customer.

I knew that Brad would probably be my recommendation to the board for our next CEO, but I didn't tell him or Wade right away. I wanted to let things play out for a while. I saw that it was difficult for Brad with me around. He and Al had made many decisions while I had been looking after Sandy. They were in the thick of the Musicland and Future Shop acquisitions. They were planning some sixty store openings in the next couple of years. They had made commitments and formed alliances. Now that I was on the scene again, though, I would be the final decision maker.

At last Brad asked me to join him for dinner. He told me he wasn't desperate to have the CEO job. He didn't want to try to out-maneuver Wade for the position. But the current situation wasn't working for him. He had a vision for the company. He could only bring it to reality as CEO.

A few years earlier, Brad had said he couldn't do his job if we didn't bring Andersen in. Then he had asked me to fire him after the consultants' master plan revealed that our operations were a mess. Now he was threatening to quit?

That dinner was the tipping point: Bradbury Anderson would be the next leader of Best Buy.

TRANSITIONS

It was a crazy start to a crazy year.

In January 2002, Maureen and I were married. It was a special day for both of us. The wedding took place at St. Thomas Aquinas Catholic Church at the University of St. Thomas, where I served as a trustee. Archbishop Harry Flynn and Father Dennis Dease performed the ceremony. Afterward, we welcomed 350 guests at the Interlachen Country Club in Edina. Maureen and I felt fortunate that we had found each other and were able to celebrate the start of a new chapter in our lives surrounded by family and friends.

Then, a month after Maureen and I were married, the company announced that I would step down as CEO and turn over the job to Brad as of June 30. The annual meeting that year, on June 26, was a memorable one. After the business portion was completed, it was farewell time. The lights dimmed. A video rolled. It showed highlights of our company's history, from our first Sound of Music store to our latest Best Buy opening.

When it was over, the audience cheered and gave me a standing ovation. And then it was my turn to speak.

"Well, as you can tell by my sideburns and the leisure suit in some of those pictures, it's been a long journey."

There was laughter.

"But what a wonderful journey it has been! I've been blessed in so many ways. I'll never be able to thank all the people who've played such a meaningful role in my life and career."

I was holding up pretty well until I came to the subject of Sandy. I talked about how I had left the company in charge of my colleagues during her illness. "The company came through like you can't believe," I said. Tears were welling in my eyes. "We've got a wonderful management team. I saw that I could give them the mantle of leadership, and they would carry it."

My voice was a little shaky. I took a moment to get myself together.

I closed by thanking everybody I could think of: our employees, my management team, our suppliers, the shareholders, the directors, and finally, my family—Sandy and my children, Maureen and her children, and all the grandchildren.

FINDING BALANCE

In that speech, I also thanked the members of the extended family that we call Best Buy. It is largely because of them that I have loved building this business so much. We are a people business, and I can't really separate my relationships with the Best Buy people from my relationship with the company.

I must admit that my intense involvement with the company and its people meant that I have not always achieved the kind of balance between my work life and my home life that Sandy would have liked. There is no question that I put a disproportionate amount of time

One of the many meetings I had with the Best Buy "family."

and energy into the company. That's just the way I'm wired. Being in the office, visiting stores, presenting to the analysts, working with the management team—all of it has been an adrenalin rush for me.

Especially in the early days when I was building the company, I was always the last person out the door. I'd spend time with anybody and everybody who needed to see me or whom I needed to see. If I bumped into somebody in the hall, it was always, *Hi, Jack! How's the family? How's the job? How is everything going?* It wasn't a management technique. I was genuinely interested, and I still am. The problem was that a simple question could easily turn into a ten-minute conversation. Then, after my conversation with Jack, I'd run into Jane: *Hi, Jane, how are you?* Meeting and talking with people is how connections get made and are kept strong. Those ties are very important to the company and are essential to its ability to grow and adapt.

However, that kind of focus on the company and the workplace can be tough on the family and home life. Many a night when I fully intended to get home by 7:00 P.M. in time for dinner, I didn't actually walk in the door until 8:15. Sandy was always understanding and accepting, but there's no doubt that she would have preferred me to be at home more than I was. My kids no doubt feel the same way.

After Sandy's death, I thought a lot about the issue of balance. I resolved to work at it and try to improve. Today, I more carefully weigh how I spend my time and where I place my interest, and am more aware of the impact of this on others. I try hard to accommodate the needs of the people around me. I really enjoy the time I spend with family and friends, as well as the time I reserve for myself— working out, attending to my philanthropic work, and looking after my other business interests. I try not to let business interfere with weekend or vacation plans. If I do spend a disproportionate amount of time at the office, I try to compensate by arranging to spend additional time with Maureen or the children and grandchildren.

Don't get me wrong: I still love the business. I have always gotten a tremendous high from my work, and I consider myself fortunate in that regard. Best Buy is an exciting place to be, and the retail industry is the most exciting of all businesses to be in. I love the never-ending challenges . . . the debates . . . the travel across the country and around the world . . . the rich agendas . . . the near-catastrophes . . . the triumphs . . . the learnings one gets from so many initiatives through so many decades.

There really is nothing like it.

GIVING BACK

Well, let me qualify that last statement.

There is another activity that I find tremendously challenging and fascinating and every bit as worthwhile as building a business. That activity is philanthropy—giving back. Today, I can spend almost as much time on my many charitable and not-for-profit activities as I do on Best Buy business.

I regret to say that it took a long time for Best Buy to be able to give back to the community in a meaningful way—about twenty-five years, in fact. That's much longer than I would have liked, but the company simply didn't have the resources to make a significant contribution.

Of course, Sandy and I always gave to the church and local charities, and the company supported the community in various ways, but the scale was small. For a long time, I felt this was a missing piece for me and for Best Buy. I believed it was unfair for us to draw from the community—bringing in revenue and making a profit—without giving back some reasonable percentage of what we had gained.

Finally, in the early 1990s, the company had grown sufficiently and was profitable enough that we could really focus on philanthropy. My daughter Susan got us started. Her son, Taylor, had some serious health problems when he was a little boy, which required him to spend a lot of time in the hospital—and, of course, Susan was there with him. During that time, she got to know many of the families who were coming through the healthcare system. She learned about the children's illnesses and the tremendous stress that families felt in dealing with them. Susan thought that Best Buy could help.

In 1992, she organized a golf tournament, worked hard to get other corporations to sponsor it alongside Best Buy, and was able to generate about $35,000, after expenses, for charity. My reaction was that the event had required a lot of effort to organize and the return was relatively small. But Susan saw the potential. She convinced Best Buy to take on sole sponsorship of the event, now called the Charity Classic, for the coming year. She threw herself into organizing it, and her efforts paid off. The 1993 charity golf event raised almost $1 million. In 1994, we formalized our efforts as the Best Buy Children's Foundation. The rest is history.

Today, the Children's Foundation raises almost $4 million annually from the Charity Classic alone. The money from this golf tournament goes to help families in communities throughout the United States, and many, many children have benefited. The Foundation has become an important part of Best Buy—an expression of our values and a manifestation of our soul.

Today, the Children's Foundation is just one of many philanthropic activities we engage in. Best Buy donates 1.5 percent of its profits to charitable causes worldwide. Wherever there is a Best Buy, you will find our employees contributing their personal time and energy to their communities. I'm very proud of the contributions we've been able to make, and I believe that we are finally giving back in a very meaningful way.

I'm sure Sandy would approve.

The Best Buy Charity Classic benefits children around the world.

CHAPTER TEN

MY TEN KEY LEARNINGS

How We Became the Best

I STEPPED DOWN AS CEO OF BEST BUY IN 2002 BUT continued on as chairman, and I have been actively—and sometimes intensely—engaged with the company throughout the past decade. During that time, we have seen a tremendous amount of success for Best Buy. Just a few of the highlights include the acquisition of Geek Squad and its phenomenal growth, our international expansion throughout Europe and Asia, and our gradual transition to a company that provides products and services for what we call the "connected world." Each of these activities, and many others, probably deserves a chapter in its own right, but I'm afraid those topics will have to wait for the next volume!

My goal for this chapter is to take a step back and talk about *how* we achieved the success we have. I have distilled the insights and experiences I have gained over the past half century into ten key learnings. Most of them I have touched upon throughout the book, but I wanted to bring them together in one chapter for easy reference. I have presented these learnings to many different audiences, both internal and external, and they seem to really resonate, so I think they are worth sharing.

1. Listen to your customers.

2. Know your competitors.

3. Perseverance pays.

4. You must have a mentor.

5. Hire strong people.

6. Learn from mistakes.

7. Leverage your strengths.

8. Be a good listener.

9. Create partnerships.

10. Innovate continuously.

These ten learnings, in conjunction with our values—which I'll discuss in the next chapter—are what have enabled us to become the best in our industry. They are as applicable and relevant today as they were when we got started back in 1966. I hope they will be useful to you, whether you are a Best Buy employee, working in some other business, or planning some future endeavor. I hope they will help you achieve the greatest success possible—both personally and professionally.

1 LISTEN TO YOUR CUSTOMERS

There's a truth about customers that most people in retail know (or should know): satisfied customers don't usually talk very much about how happy they are with the product they bought, the service they received, or the store they visited. You can do five things right for them, and they won't offer a word about it unless someone asks them directly. Customers expect everything to go well—as they should.

Do one thing wrong, however, and you're in trouble—although you may be the last to know it. Customers won't always tell *you* about the problem, but they will talk. Believe me, they'll talk. They will tell at least five other people about their dissatisfaction. They'll go into agonizing detail. They'll embellish the story. So you have to do everything humanly possible to be sure the customer really *is* satisfied. One important way to do that is to ask questions and listen to what the customer has to tell you.

Let me share a story that illustrates this point.

Not long ago, as I was visiting a Best Buy store, I bumped into a retired Catholic priest—someone I know very well. He was on his way out, empty-handed.

"Hello, Father," I said.

"Oh, Dick, hello!" he replied. He looked a little sheepish, as if he really didn't want to talk to me.

I sensed something was not right. We chatted for a moment, and then I asked what had brought him to Best Buy.

"Oh, I was thinking about buying a flat-screen TV," he said.

"Did you find what you wanted?" I asked.

The retired priest looked uncomfortable. "Well, yes," he said. "I found the model I was looking for, but uh . . ."

"Was there something about it you didn't like?" I asked. "Did we fall short in some way?"

"No, I liked the TV," he protested. "And the salesperson was perfectly helpful and everything. I just need to think about it a little bit."

"What is it you need to think about, if you don't mind my asking?" I said.

Finally, he came out with it. "It's just that your price is a little high, that's all, Dick."

"Really?" I did not like the sound of this.

"Yes. In fact, the exact same model is twenty dollars less next door at Costco."

"Twenty dollars less?"

"That's right."

"Well, Father," I said. "I'm sure we can make an adjustment for you." I steered him back into the store and called the manager over. "The good father here tells me that the TV he'd like to buy is twenty dollars cheaper at Costco," I said.

The manager looked uneasy. "Really?" he said. "Well, I'll check into that right away." He made a move toward his computer.

"Good," I said, "but I'm quite sure we can trust that we are being told the truth. So before you check into the price, let's see if we can make an adjustment for him right now."

"Oh, of course," said the manager. The price was adjusted, the sale was made, and the good father went on his way, happy.

I was not so happy. I took the manager aside. "How is it that we are twenty dollars higher on this TV than the guys next door?" I asked.

"Well, we charge more because we do more," he said. "The customer knows that. We have a greater range of products. We have a deeper assortment. We offer better service."

"OK, but why are we twenty dollars higher?" I asked again.

"Because we make more profit that way." The manager looked at me as if I had lost my touch.

"We don't make *any* profit if we don't make the sale," I said.

The manager looked at me blankly. He didn't seem to be getting my point.

"How was this pricing decision made?" I asked.

"At the district level," the manager said. "All the stores in the district sell that TV at the same price."

After I left the store, I called the district manager. I told him about the priest and the premium-priced TV.

The DM knew all about it. "Sure, we've been looking for ways to maximize profitability," he said. "On certain items, we display a higher price. If the customer challenges it, the store manager has the authority to make an adjustment. But if the customer hasn't shopped around, we get the higher margin."

"Hasn't shopped around?" I said. "What customer doesn't shop around? *Everybody* shops around. Nobody comes in the store without having looked on the Internet or checked the competitor across the street."

"Well . . . ," the DM mumbled.

"And if they buy our product at the higher price and find out later they could have gotten it for twenty bucks less, then what happens?" I continued. "They're going to tell their friends. And their friends will tell their friends. You might lose them all as customers forever. It's up to us to make sure the customer is winning."

"OK, but what about all the extras we offer?" the DM asked. "There's a lot of value there."

"Those are tie-breakers," I said. "Sure, they have value. Yes, the customer appreciates them. It's our hope the extras may even convince the customer to buy from us rather than the other guys. *But not if they cost one dollar extra.* The customer wants the lowest price *and* the highest value. That's what 'best buy' means. We put that name over the door for a very good reason."

OK, let me calm down for a second.

The point of the story is that we are not involved in a game with our customer. Our goal is *not* to make them lose so we can win. We want them to win so we can win, too. Listening to them is necessary. And acting on what they say is essential.

Any questions?

2 KNOW YOUR COMPETITORS

In the consumer electronics industry, competition was fierce at the end of the 1980s. The challenge for any business in our industry was to differentiate itself from its competitors. At the time, we thought the only way to do that was on price. We slashed our cost of doing business and hung in there. But when you have very little margin, you don't have much room to maneuver. We knew that the low-cost approach was not a game we could win over the long term.

Instead, we had to rewrite the rules somehow—break away from the pack of look-alike competitors. As early as the tornado sale in 1981, we caught a glimpse of a new direction in sales. We saw that our customers wanted a very different experience than our competitors were offering. They wanted:

- A hassle-free shopping experience.
- No haggling over price.
- A big selection at lower prices.
- Quick and easy checkout.
- Accurate information on products.
- Service after the sale.

We knew that our competitors in the consumer electronics industry were not delivering this experience, and that gave us a huge opportunity. Based on that understanding, we made two bold moves. First, we redesigned our stores for a brighter, more open, fun and friendly feel; we called it Concept II. Concept II enabled us to make up for our lower margins with huge volume and to enhance our profitability by offering services that our competitors didn't.

The second bold move: we took our sales staff off commission and put them on salary. We found that the old adage is true: People don't like to be sold, but they love to buy. Customers loved the new approach.

We took a calculated risk that our competitors would not follow us in this direction, at least not right away. That's because we knew them so well. We understood their cost structure and their selling tactics. We doubted they had the interest or the will to transform themselves. We believed that they would continue to put their own needs before those of the customer.

All these years later, the risk we took with Concept II has clearly paid off. *All* those competitors have disappeared, because they were unwilling or unable to change their business model.

Now, however, we have a whole new set of competitors to contend with—including the general merchandisers and online retailers—and it's our job to understand them and know how they operate. If we have to make another bold move to differentiate ourselves from them, we'll do so.

3 PERSEVERANCE PAYS

Often, the only way to achieve success when you're a young company is through sheer, hard-headed determination.

After founding Sound of Music, I put in seventeen years of hard work with only modest success. In some of those years, we were just hanging on, trying to survive. More than once, we came close to bankruptcy. What kept us going? A dogged determination to provide what the customer wanted. A constant search for the best, most unique way to develop a business niche and serve it to the best of our ability.

Entrepreneurship requires perseverance. It's certainly not for everybody. There's no rulebook. It's fraught with risk. There will be setbacks and disappointments and periods of uncertainty. To endure all that, you have to totally believe in your mission and be completely convinced that, over the long term, you're going to win. Even in our shakiest times at Best Buy, I never accepted the possibility of failure. I believed that we were on the right track and that our customers would always understand we were on their side. Through it all, we persevered.

Today, we're facing new challenges. We can't expect or hope they will go away. We can't be daunted when we hit a bump in the road. With an unshakeable belief in our mission, unyielding perseverance, and the ability to adapt, we will continue to add to our long record of successes.

YOU MUST HAVE A MENTOR

4 As important as it is to believe in your mission, you also have to keep in touch with reality. That's where a good mentor comes in. A mentor helps keep you grounded. A mentor helps you put your successes and your failures in perspective. When you start to believe you can do no wrong, your mentor can let you know just how wrong you are about that. When you come up against a tough issue, a mentor helps you think outside the box. Ideally, a mentor has traveled a similar path and can act as your guide.

In my experience, the best mentor is a person who is:

- Actively engaged in a business, or recently retired from a successful career.
- Genuinely interested in you personally and able to really connect with you.
- Knowledgeable about your industry.
- A good fit for the business you're working to build. You can't expect a Fortune 50 executive to mentor you if you're still at $10 million in revenue. Nor do you want the leader of a small company as a mentor if you're running a global enterprise.

We would not be the company we are today if it weren't for my mentor, Ezra "Zeke" Landres, God rest his soul. Zeke did all the things a mentor should do. He forced me to look carefully at what Best Buy was and to think hard about what the company could become. Zeke's mentoring, which came at a critical time in our development, was an important factor in my becoming a better leader.

I should add that mentoring is not only about individuals mentoring one another; it must also become an institutional activity. That's why we established the Best Buy Leadership Institute—as a way to formalize the transfer of our management practices and core values from one generation to the next.

In order for our employees to perform at a best-in-class level and to take on greater leadership responsibilities, they have to think hard about the nature of leadership. What is required of a leader in today's rapidly changing business environment? What are the best ways to encourage and motivate employees? What are the best ways to build a high-performing team? How do our values play out in our day-to-day work in the stores?

You cannot learn these things just by reading about them or even through a good in-store training program. You need to interact with senior executives, with education experts, and with peers throughout the company. So, in our leadership development efforts, we bring leaders together—both at headquarters and at venues around the country—to engage one another. They talk about challenges, successes, and problems. They learn new concepts, are exposed to the latest management thinking, and discuss new practices. They share solutions, surface opportunities, and discuss how to apply what they have learned to their work. They discuss, debate, and tell stories. They get into the good, the bad, and the ugly. We all gain tremendous benefit from their sharing of learnings.

Here's a story that I believe illustrates this learning well. It comes from Stephanie Stitch-Durbin, who began with Best Buy as a cashier and is now GM, Store 141.

"My story starts in a small town in California. In 2004, I lost my job, got divorced, and had a car accident—all in the space of thirty days. I needed work badly, so I applied for a job as a cashier at Best Buy.

Orientation was fun and exciting and for the first time in a long time, I felt like I belonged to something. It was more than a business, more than a team, it was family. I fell in love.

Over the next nine months I received three promotions and realized that I wanted to become a general manager. After a false start as a sales manager, I took an assignment that proved to be the most challenging of my career. I became the product process manager in a severely challenged, urban store. It had high shrink, ineffective systems, and homeless people sleeping in the vestibule. During my first week there, an entire trailer was stolen off the loading dock, product and all.

When I was selected for the job, I was told that I needed more 'edge.' I am a person who feeds off positive energy, and loves to develop people and see them grow. But I also like to win. I decided that I could show edge (as I understood it) as well as anybody. I challenged, chastised, and confronted my way through the day.

Then I was selected to participate in a leadership development program. One part of it involved getting feedback from one's employees. I received eighty-seven comments. All of them bad.

'I don't want to come to work when she's there.'
'She's always yelling at people.'
'She never smiles.'

I thought hard about the comments. 'How did I fall so far from grace? Was it so bad that I would have to leave Best

Buy?' That possibility made my eyes fill with tears. Best Buy had been the one thing that I could really be proud of. Was it about to be over?

Not long after I received the feedback, the human resources manager for our district came to see me. He knew all about what had happened.

'That was rough feedback you got,' he said. 'I was amazed at how well you handled it. It takes a strong person to go through that and maintain composure.'

It was all I could do to keep from completely melting down. Then my HR manager told me that he had gone through a similar experience early in his career, but that a mentor had helped him find the way. We talked a lot about the role of a leader and he gave me a wonderful book about the importance of leadership.

I learned something important that day. I may have had a lot of enemies, but at least I had somebody in my corner. That's all anyone needs to be inspired—to have one person who believes in them.

Over the next few months I had a rebirth as a leader. Developing people became my priority. I spent lots of time talking with employees and became their 'go-to' leader. When another evaluation was done, the feedback was all positive.

Then, at last, a general manager position opened up. I knew in my heart it was the store for me. Ten people applied for the job. I got it. The pinnacle moment in my interview was the heartfelt story of my painful struggle and miraculous turnaround.

After a couple of years, I had a chance to return the favor my HR manager had given me. One of my managers received some devastating feedback from an employee. The manager was concerned that I wouldn't understand. I shared my story with him and gave him a copy of the book that helped me so much. I believe I helped save his career, just as my HR manager had saved mine."

Isn't it amazing what an effect a mentor can have on an individual, a career, and a company?

5 HIRE STRONG PEOPLE

Entrepreneurs, and plenty of executives, are notorious for not hiring strong people. That's because we tend to believe that we've got all the answers, and we don't really want to be challenged as much as we need to be. Please, don't kid yourself. Every entrepreneur, every executive, and every manager needs strong people around them. As I learned from our engagement with Andersen Consulting, those strong people may have to include some outsiders—consultants,

Hire strong people and listen to them.

partners, and advisers. You always need to have access to the best people—those who have the necessary skills and the ability to perform at the highest level.

If you refuse to hire people as strong or stronger than you are, your success will be limited. So you have no choice but to go after the best people. In a competitive job environment, of course, there is tremendous competition for top talent. You cannot expect that you are such a charismatic person in such a fantastic company that everyone will be begging to work for you. You will have to make a strong case for your company, your business, and your plans for the future.

At Best Buy, while we work hard to bring in good people from outside, we deeply believe in hiring and promoting from within. Here, you can start out as a store employee and end up as CEO— Brad and Brian are both proof of that. Many of our store general managers began as cashiers. They intended to leave the company as soon as they could find a "real job"—but found the job with us so rewarding, they never left. Because we so strongly believe in promoting from within, we put a lot of emphasis on bringing the right people into the company in the first place. Time and time again, we have seen that Best Buy is a company where ordinary people can achieve extraordinary things—every day.

6 LEARN FROM MISTAKES

At Best Buy, our culture encourages and rewards innovation. Because innovation involves trying new things, it has a higher failure rate than the execution of proven strategies does. That's why it's very important to create a culture that does not punish people for making mistakes. We view mistakes as an investment in employee training—assuming, of course, that the person and the company learn from the mistake and share what has been learned with others.

At Best Buy, we have made our share of mistakes. As you'll remember, one of the most dramatic was the year that one of our merchants purchased a huge number of personal computers that were about to become obsolete. Yes, he made a miscalculation, but not a stupid or careless one. His intention was right: he wanted to have enough inventory on hand to satisfy customer demand during the holiday season.

The point is, we learned a lot from that experience, and the company ultimately benefited. We made significant changes in how we managed inventory. Those changes propelled us into an incredible growth spurt and led to a significant improvement in profitability.

We will never eliminate mistakes, so it's essential that we learn from them. We have to look carefully at every mistake, determine what caused it, and figure out how to keep it from happening again. If we don't get at the root cause of the mistake, it can become institutionalized and happen over and over again. That can really be a problem and can limit our success. So, while we shouldn't punish mistakes, we also have to summon the courage to call them out when we see them.

It's also important to say that we don't want to *encourage* mistakes or tolerate those that could reasonably have been avoided. That's where performance management comes in. Winning companies focus on results and reward the people who deliver them.

7 LEVERAGE YOUR STRENGTHS

Throughout this book, I've told stories and talked about events that enabled me to understand people better. One thing I've learned over the years is just how differently people approach situations and issues. Even in a group of like-minded folks, it's amazing how different their thinking can be. Each person has a unique perspective, distinctive strengths, and characteristic ways of meeting challenges. These differences are what make us individuals, and we should celebrate them.

I believe you get the best from people by recognizing their differences and focusing on their strengths rather than pointing out their shortcomings. Most of us want to do a good job and are well aware of our weaknesses. In order to improve our performance and be valued by our colleagues, most of us will try to improve ourselves as much as we can.

As much as possible, we at Best Buy want to place people in positions where their strengths are maximized. We especially want to encourage the entrepreneurial spirit in everyone—the desire to grow, try new things, innovate, and constantly improve. When people inside a large organization act like entrepreneurs we call them "intrapreneurs."

Although we usually think of leveraging strengths as a way for people to move up in the organization, it doesn't always play out that way. Sometimes it's about people being asked to use different "muscles" than the ones normally required for their jobs—and finding that they have strength there as well.

Here's a story from Marc Gordon, who is now VP of Finance, about an episode when he was asked to use a very different set of strengths—quite literally—in order to get some important work done.

"I started work with Best Buy in the summer of 1993 as an accountant. One of the many things that attracted me to the company was an impending move of headquarters to a beautiful new corporate campus in Eden Prairie.

As the fall of 1993 approached, however, we were told we would not be moving to the new campus until the following

January. We were disappointed about the delay, but we soon found that it created an interesting opportunity.

Turns out that the reason for the delay was that the new facility was going to be used as warehouse space to deal with a bigger-than-expected holiday demand. And what's more, the temporary warehouse needed temporary workers, too. Many of us who pushed pencils for a living were now going to be pushing pallets instead!

We dressed down and reported for work. Our assignment was to repack products from large cases to smaller boxes. It was a lot of fun. All hands on deck. Everybody working together for a common purpose. It was a great way for the accountants to experience a part of retail operations that was foreign to many of us.

We eventually made the move to Eden Prairie and, over the years, I've had the chance to leverage my strengths in other ways. But I will never forget those days in 1993. Not only was the work fun and necessary, it gave me the chance to brush up on my pallet-handling skills. You never know when they might come in handy again."

I really love that story. Who would have guessed that a group of accountants could have gained so much from pushing pallets around? I believe that companies that fail to leverage the strengths of their people, in whatever way is necessary, get themselves in trouble. That's what happened to Circuit City, Highland, and Montgomery Ward. Their leaders thought they had all the answers and failed to pay enough attention to the people around them.

At Best Buy, we have always tried to leverage the strengths of our people. When we succeed at doing so, the energy generated is amazing. Our people feel it, and so do our customers.

8 BE A GOOD LISTENER

The single best lesson I have learned in my years of leadership—and probably the most painful one—is how important it is to be a good listener. Like the other learnings, I came to this one through a memorable personal experience.

In the early days, we often conducted management get-togethers that we called "symposiums." The purpose was to come up with solutions to urgent challenges we were facing. I remember one of those sessions very well. About a hundred Best Buy people attended. They were all very talented, productive, well-compensated, successful people. They had responsibility for all the major activities of the company, including store management, distribution, service, human resources, and information technology.

We began in a group session. The facilitator wrote a challenge on the whiteboard. We talked about it for a while and then broke into groups of about eight people each. We had sixty minutes to come up with solutions to the challenge.

What happened in my group completely blew me away. After we had reviewed the issue for a few minutes, we turned to brainstorming. Instantly, everybody looked to me. I was CEO, after all. They expected me to go first. I tossed out six or seven ways that we could address the issue at hand. The group leader scribbled them on the whiteboard. I had a few more ideas, but I kept them in reserve, just in case we got bogged down later. Truthfully, I figured I had pretty much covered the waterfront. I doubted the group would come up with many more solutions.

Wrong. As soon as I shut up, everybody else started throwing out ideas. Thirty minutes later, my seven solutions had ballooned to thirty. All of them were substantial and meaningful, and added dimensions and nuances that I had not considered.

I couldn't believe how naive I had been. I had assumed that, since I was the CEO and had been with the company the longest, I would naturally be the one with the best answers. Far from it. My ideas were good but hardly the complete or final word.

That's when I began to see just how much I would have missed if people had not been given the opportunity to speak—and if I had not listened closely to what they had to say. Most people want to make a difference to their company and community. They want to play a useful role in achieving a successful outcome. They just need a chance to do so. Listen to them!

Listening cannot hurt you, but refusing to listen surely will.

9 CREATE PARTNERSHIPS
Who are we? Who is Best Buy?

It's easy to think of Best Buy as nothing more, and nothing less, than the sum total of its employees. At the Best Buy Corporate Campus in Richfield, Minnesota, you will find up to four thousand people at any given time. Are we the four thousand smartest people on the planet? Probably not. On our own, do we have all the necessary talents and skills to make our business go? No way. There are nearly 180,000 more people in Best Buy stores, service centers, warehouses, and other locations around the world. Do they represent all the talent and power of Best Buy? Do they bring to the table everything we need to succeed? Negative.

Best Buy is a community made up of four main constituencies: employees, customers, vendors, and shareholders. All four groups are important and necessary to the success of the company. All four must work together, in partnership, if Best Buy is to succeed.

Everything we do, every decision we make, needs to create a winning outcome for all four constituencies. If we take advantage of one group over another, the relationship will not be sustainable. The disadvantaged group won't tolerate being short-changed for very long. They will resort to whatever tactic is necessary to improve their position. That constituency will compromise the enterprise and may even try to disadvantage our position. But if all four groups see they are winning, the enterprise as a whole wins.

To create winning outcomes for the customer, for example, we have made a number of acquisitions. To improve our service offering, we acquired and developed Geek Squad. To extend our offering to customers around the world, we bought Future Shop in Canada and Five Star Appliance in China. To extend our product offerings into new areas, we bought exciting brands like Magnolia, Pacific Sales, and Carphone Warehouse.

In order to offer certain kinds of services that relate to our products, but that we are not able or do not wish to provide, we have developed many corporate partnerships—with vendors like Comcast, Time Warner, Netflix, and Direct TV. Such partnerships enable us not only to improve the customer experience but also to reward our shareholders, because we avoid taking on the expense of developing such services ourselves.

So, while we know that our employees are essential to our success, we also need to keep in mind the importance of good relationships among all four constituencies.

10 INNOVATE CONTINUOUSLY

What do I mean by *continuous innovation*? I mean very simply that innovation is not an optional activity. It's not something we'll get around to when we have the time. It's not something that only a few of us need to do. It's not something we can outsource or leave to a consultant.

Innovation must be a central part of the way we do business. Foundational retail execution is the price of admission in our industry—and is the key to what has made us so successful. But great execution is not enough to keep us in our current position. We must be able to execute brilliantly and, *at the same time*, constantly think about what we can and should be doing differently and better.

How do we do this? How do we slug it out in a fast-moving and competitive environment—and also innovate continuously? It's really a matter of being curious. Always being on the lookout for things that could be improved. Challenging ourselves to do better, every day. Challenging our colleagues to do the same. Being willing to stretch ourselves.

All these things add up to an innovation mind-set. It is through innovation that we will differentiate Best Buy from our competitors, attract customers, and keep our talented employees engaged and committed. It is the job of our leaders to model the innovation mind-set and to create an environment where innovation is nurtured.

Part of the innovation mind-set is understanding how to build on a new idea when it shows promise—and knowing what to do if it isn't working. That requires getting tough about testing and evaluating new ideas. When the results demonstrate that the idea has real potential, don't sit on it! Share it. Find ways to improve and grow it. Get it out to other departments, categories, customers, or markets.

What if the evaluation shows that the idea is probably a dud? The first thing to recognize is that failure is not only tolerable in the innovation process, it's necessary. In fact, if we are not failing often, that likely means we're not stretching ourselves, not pushing the envelope hard enough.

The key is to fail fast. Failing fast frees up time and energy to apply to the next, hopefully better, idea. And when there is failure, don't hide it. Learn from it. Share what you learn from the failure with others throughout the company, so their efforts will have a better chance of success.

We have always had a culture of innovation at Best Buy. Today, however, we need to take our innovation efforts to a whole new level. We must challenge ourselves to rethink, reinvent, and reimagine what we do.

The effort has to be company-wide. Everyone can, and must, play a role in innovation. I don't care what your position is or whether you think of yourself as creative. Very few people can come up with big, brilliant, new ideas. Many of us can, however, come up with smart ideas for improvements, refinements, extensions, and new applications for existing approaches.

Sometimes these ideas lead to internal process improvements; sometimes they can generate whole new business activities. Best Buy for Business, for example, grew out of an idea generated by two employees, Al Keenan and Todd Larson. Their insight was that small businesses had very distinct needs when it came to electronic components, software, and other products and services that we sell. Businesses have different product performance requirements than consumers do; their service needs are different; and their buying habits differ as well. Why not create a separate unit just to cater to them? The result is Best Buy for Business, which provides commercial-grade products coupled with account management services that businesses want but consumers don't need—like bulk ordering and flexible payment options. Today, Best Buy for Business serves more than 35,000 customers each year, employs 450 people, and, from 2007 to 2011, exceeded $1.7 billion in revenue.

That's just one terrific example of organic growth through innovation—that is, innovation that bubbles up from inside the organization. It's proof that ideas can come from anyone, anywhere in the organization. What's more, you don't have to come up with the original spark in order to play a meaningful role in the innovation process. There are many roles to play in bringing an idea to life. Some people may shine at communicating the idea. Others may find they have the knack of creating the right partnerships to apply it. These may be seen as supporting roles in the innovation process, but we need them, too. This is the philosophy behind the Chairman's Innovation Award program, which recognizes and rewards employees in primary and supporting roles who participate in innovation projects that demonstrate value.

So don't leave innovation to others. Everyone can be involved!

LEARNINGS ARE INVALUABLE, BUT THEY'RE NOT EVERYTHING

I truly believe in the ten key learnings I have described in this chapter and throughout the book. I also know that they are not enough, by themselves, to make Best Buy—or any company that might choose to follow them—successful over the long term.

The other essential ingredient is, of course, values. Without strong values—well articulated and constantly modeled by a company's leadership—even the best execution on the ten learnings will not be enough. It is values that drive a company, help us make the right decisions, and enable us to remain flexible and capable of creating positive change when change is necessary.

You don't need very many values. They don't have to be complicated. They don't even have to be particularly original. They do, however, have to be genuine. They have to be believed. And, as we'll see in the next chapter, they have to be lived and practiced, every day.

CHAPTER ELEVEN

VALUES

Our Secret Sauce

TOGETHER, WE HAVE BUILT ONE OF THE GREATEST companies on earth. I am incredibly proud of what we have accomplished and of who we are today. There is no limit to what we can achieve in the future, if we successfully create opportunities for ourselves and seize the ones that come our way.

There is a serious challenge we have to be mindful of, however. It's a challenge that has gotten the better of many successful companies and troubled a lot of talented company leaders. I'm referring to the issue of *great size* and all the problems that come along with an organization as big as ours: bureaucracy, turf battles, complicated processes, lack of speed, and more.

You might say, *Well, doesn't size bring advantages, too? What's wrong with scale and buying power and clout and brand recognition?* Yes, those are all good things. But gorilla size also has some monster drawbacks.

Drawback number one is adaptability, or lack thereof. Being a battleship is great when you're cruising full steam ahead on a vast ocean, but changing course is another matter altogether. You turn the wheel, and nothing much happens until you're five miles along.

Meanwhile, smaller craft are racing by you. Suddenly, you're the follower, not the leader.

Drawback number two is invincibility, or belief in same. *Hey, we're Best Buy! We've got billions in assets! We're in the Fortune 50! Nothing can bring us down! We are* invincible! Wrong. Let me offer a little perspective on the Fortune 500 list. First published in 1955, it tracks the largest and most stable companies in the United States. Getting on the list is hard. Staying there is even harder. Of the hundred companies at the top of the list in 1980, just a little over thirty years ago, *seventy-four of them are gone*—out of business, sold, swallowed up, kaput. Those companies thought they were battleships, but they turned out to be *Titanic*s. They sank, sometimes really fast.

Now here's the good news: Twenty-six of the one hundred companies on the list in 1980 are still there—names like Wal-Mart, IBM, Procter & Gamble, Microsoft, General Electric, Coca-Cola, and Walt Disney. They're the ones that figured out how to deal with the challenge of being big. They learned how to adapt and stay nimble. They found ways to combat the delusion of invincibility. If Best Buy wants to stay on the list, we have to do the same.

How do we do that?

Well, of course, we have to execute brilliantly on all the things we do every day to make sure the business is going full steam ahead. But, as important as great execution is, *it's not enough*. Strong execution can bring about terrific short-term results, but it won't guarantee long-term success. For that, you have to have values. And not only do you have to have values, you have to live by them, make decisions in light of them, evaluate performance by them, and communicate constantly about them.

That's why I'm making such a point of devoting an entire chapter to the discussion of values. There is no question in my mind that the secret sauce of our past success has been values and the compelling culture that is distinctively Best Buy. I am equally certain that our values will be the secret sauce of our success in the future. It is values that have differentiated Best Buy from our competitors over the past forty-plus years. They set us apart now. Most important, they will make us different and distinctive in the future, as new competitors come on the scene.

It's especially important for large companies to place a strong emphasis on values because of the great diversity within their organizations and the constant flow of people into and around the company. Small companies don't usually state their values explicitly, because they don't really have to. We didn't when we were Sound of Music. We didn't have to write them down or make a big deal about them. We didn't even really think about them. They were just there. We modeled them. Everybody could see them in action.

When Best Buy started to take off in the 1980s, however, everything changed. As we opened stores on the West Coast, in the deep South, in New York, and in New England, we realized that we were very Midwestern in our views. We had a strong belief in the value of hard work, deep faith, ethics, and integrity. But now we were no longer a Midwestern company. No longer did everybody know everybody else. Our employees came from many different backgrounds. We had city folks and country folks—people from different religious and cultural backgrounds, from all kinds of family situations, and with different educational histories. We could no longer assume that everybody knew or understood the values of the company. Nor could we assume that we understood how they thought and felt, or what they believed.

We said, "Wow, we need to set up some rules of the road. We have to establish some guidelines and put them out there so everyone's on the same page, whether they're working at the Edina store, at headquarters, in Texas, in Mexico, or wherever they may be."

That's the purpose of our values statements. But it's important to realize that they're not just statements, not just nice phrases suitable for framing. Our managers think about these values as they consider their plans and actions. All employees are evaluated by them. And we have even gone so far as to develop a process that enables employees to call out leaders who they believe are *not* living and leading by the values.

With all of this discussion of the values, you might think they would be long, complicated, and somehow grand. Wrong. As every Best Buy employee knows, there are only four values, and none of them is longer than six words. Here they are:

> *Have fun while being the best.*
> *Learn from challenge and change.*
> *Show respect, humility, and integrity.*
> *Unleash the power of our people.*

Simple. Easy to remember. And true.

With them, we can overcome any obstacle, meet any challenge. Without them . . . game over.

I'm not exaggerating about this. I strongly believe that our future success depends on our ability to live our values. Period.

Now let's look at the values, one by one, in a little more detail.

HAVE FUN WHILE BEING THE BEST

It's very easy to tell when people in a company are *not* having fun. And just as easy to see when they are.

I'll never forget a visit I made to the headquarters of one of our suppliers—a big corporation, a well-known Fortune 500 name. This company was big, and it was struggling. It wasn't growing. It wasn't innovating. Its market share was dropping. Its reputation was slipping.

I could tell all that from one look at their headquarters. The top brass had big offices with big windows. The managers had small offices with small windows. The staff had cubicles with no windows. There was very little conversation. No laughter. No excitement or infectious energy. Many of the offices were empty. Every desktop was tidy as could be.

The place gave me the willies. Where were the whiteboards filled with ideas? Where were the conversations and debates and arguments? Where was the mess and the excitement of collaboration and innovation? I have never forgotten that image. It was a dying company, and you could see and feel it everywhere.

It should be fun and engaging to come to work.

Our company headquarters and my family office, where we handle our personal investments and philanthropic activities, are both beehives of activity. I keep throwing new challenges at the staff. They snap them up and introduce new ideas for consideration. There is not a lot of sitting at a desk.

The same is true in our stores. When we cast right, our people *want* to come to work. Why wouldn't they? They get to engage with products and activities they love. They teach customers and learn from them. They work with people whom they like and who like them. Is every customer interaction a joy? No. Does every conversation fuel passion? No. But every one of them offers an opportunity to learn and grow.

When I walk into a Best Buy store anywhere in the world, I can see the excitement and passion on the faces of employees and customers. I can hear it in the tone of the conversations. Having fun is infectious. It rubs off on people. It creates good outcomes for everyone.

But don't forget the "being the best" part of this value. Like unbridled passion, fun without the discipline of excellence creates chaos. No one wins.

Have fun. Be the best. We all win.

LEARN FROM CHALLENGE AND CHANGE

Fun is important. Learning is equally so.

People get genuinely charged up by taking action and assuming responsibilities that teach them new things. Winners like to learn more about the subjects and endeavors they already know—about music, photography, cooking, movies, or computers. They also want to learn about new things that will help them prepare for their next steps in life—about management, teamwork, psychology, consumer behavior, merchandising, and communications.

At Best Buy, learning means much more than on-the-job training. We want our people to be successful, period! We hope that their success will be with Best Buy, and that they'll stay with us for a long time to come. We invest in them. They invest in us. We work hard to create a winning relationship, a long-term partnership.

But if it doesn't work out—if there is no space for a person to grow and succeed at Best Buy in the way they want to—we wish them success wherever they go. My desire is that everybody who leaves Best Buy walks out a smarter person than when they walked in. It's our job to create the right opportunities for them to succeed. If not, it's as much our fault as it is theirs.

Today, learning is more important than it has ever been. We're operating in a business environment that changes constantly and rapidly. When business conditions are this fluid and dynamic, no company and no employee can stand still for very long. We have to change, too, and changing means thinking and behaving in new ways.

Human beings don't change instantly, however, and they don't make a change all by themselves. They have to learn about the change. They have to understand *why* a change is being made, *why* it's important to the company, *why* it's important to them personally.

So many *whys*! It reminds me of my granddaughter, Chelsea. When she was about five years old, she started asking the *Why?*

question. One summer afternoon at our lake home, Chelsea was sitting on my lap while I read her a story. I'd read a little bit and she'd ask, "Why did that happen, Grandpa?"

I'd give her the best explanation I could think of. Then I'd read some more.

"Why did he do that, Grandpa?"

I'd explain, then read another sentence or two.

"Why did she say that, Grandpa?"

Finally, I got impatient. At the next *Why?* I replied, "Because I said so, Chelsea!"

That response didn't satisfy Chelsea, and it won't work for employees either. Although it is necessary for businesses to *think* in a *revolutionary* way, a large company needs to *act* in an *evolutionary* way. You can't slam-dunk a major change through a big organization. You have to plan and evolve your way into and through it.

People are used to doing what they do and doing it in ways they have learned and perfected. If, all of a sudden, they are asked to change certain aspects of what they do, there will be confusion and resistance. But that resistance is rarely a result of stubbornness. It usually comes about because the importance of the situation— the big picture—has not been communicated properly. It hasn't been explained. It hasn't been taught. And therefore it hasn't been understood.

So when we introduce a new strategy, concept, or objective, we have to explain it completely. We have to answer all the *whys*: Why are we going in this direction? Why is this innovation initiative so important? Why are we doing things in a new way, when we're doing great the way things are?

Change is such an important part of our lives today that every manager has to be a teacher. Managers need to help people understand the new way, whatever it is. They need to listen to endless questions and provide good answers. If they don't know the answer to a question, it's their job to search for an answer. They need to achieve buy-in so that each member of the team knows his or her role in the new direction or idea.

Thank you, Chelsea, for that important lesson.

SHOW RESPECT, HUMILITY, AND INTEGRITY

Most people think of themselves as respectful, humble, and full of integrity. But exactly what do those characteristics mean? What do they look like in practice? Different people can interpret them very differently. That's why it's important to use language that makes these values explicit—and why it's absolutely essential to model them in our behaviors. The rules of the road apply to everyone, from the CEO to the newest employee anywhere in the Best Buy enterprise.

Brad Anderson taught me a lot about these values. You may have wondered about Brad's path from commissioned salesperson to his management job at headquarters. When and how did he make the leap? Well, the story says a lot about Brad's qualities of respect, humility, and integrity.

You may remember that Brad started as a salesperson in our West St. Paul store in 1973. In 1980, after he had been with the company for nearly eight years, I was looking for a person who could take on the role of district manager. One day, I stopped by the West St. Paul store. I found Brad in the parking lot, watching as one of his employees climbed into the trunk of a car to install a car stereo system.

I was acquainted with Brad, but I didn't know him really well. I certainly didn't know what his personal ambitions were. I guess I assumed that he was content as a store manager. After we had chatted for a few minutes, I told Brad that I was looking to hire a new district manager.

"Brad," I asked. "Have you seen anybody from headquarters that you think might be good for this position? The person has to be highly competent, capable, and trustworthy. It must be someone who really embodies our values and who can talk to employees in the stores on behalf of the company. Somebody with a lot of integrity. Not a showboat."

Brad thought for a moment or two. He seemed to be struggling for an answer. "I guess I just don't know what to say," he said finally.

"Really?" This surprised me. "You mean nobody has made a real positive impression on you?"

"To tell the truth, no," he said at last. "The people that I've seen from headquarters don't seem very savvy about what goes on in the field. They don't show us much respect or really seem to care what our opinions are." Brad didn't seem very comfortable with this conversation and kept watching the installer while we talked.

"So you don't think we have anybody in the company who would be good for a management role?" I asked.

Finally Brad turned to me and looked me right in the eye. "Yes, we do," he said with great conviction.

"Great," I said. "Who is it?"

"Me," he said.

I had never thought of Brad as a senior manager. "Really? You're interested in being a district manager?"

"I think I know how to make things happen," Brad said. "I've been in the field. I have my experience here at the store. I think I can really help the company ferret out what's bad and promote what's good."

Something about the way Brad said that—his straightforward and honest manner—impressed me. And even though he spoke with confidence, he wasn't arrogant. There was humility in his tone.

He kept going. "I'm not fancy, but I can tell right from wrong, good from bad, and I think I can do this job as well as—if not better than—anybody."

I wasn't prepared to respond on the spot. "Let me give it some thought," I said.

Brad nodded, and we shook hands.

I drove away scratching my head. *Would anybody follow this guy? Would they listen to him?* Brad hardly looked like the kind of take-charge individual I thought I was seeking. Still, he had presented himself strongly. And he had done a good job managing the store. He had always acted with integrity. He was a humble person. He always spoke with respect for others. I decided to bring him to headquarters to see what he could do.

The rest is history. Brad has always been one of our best models of the important qualities of respect, humility, and integrity.

UNLEASH THE POWER OF OUR PEOPLE

There may be danger in being big, but there is also unbelievable power in it.

There is almost no limit to the amount of energy and number of ideas that can be generated by a company of 180,000 people. The key, however, is to find ways to unleash that power. In too many companies, management wants to retain too much control. Rather than empower their people, they put them in handcuffs. Rather than listen to them, they lecture them.

The power of a large company resides in its people. The people provide the adrenalin the enterprise needs to succeed. They fuel its innovation. They determine the next steps the company must take.

At Best Buy, much of that energy comes from the largest group of employees, the 120,000 blue shirts who engage with customers in our stores around the world every day. They are the public face of

The Best Buy blue shirt represents service, product knowledge, and passion.

Best Buy, and from their ranks come a large percentage of our managers and executives.

We introduced the blue shirt in 1989, and over the years, it has taken on incredible significance both inside the company and out. Today, the blue shirt helps set us apart from our competitors. Customers know about our blue shirts and understand what they represent: service, helpfulness, product knowledge, problem solving, enthusiasm. They may not remember the name of the person who gave them great service, but they always remember that he or she was proudly wearing Best Buy blue.

It's incredibly important to the enterprise that our blue shirts— as well as our yellow shirts in greeting and security, our black or white shirts in service, and our management team everywhere—are winning. That means, for starters, that we have to get the basics right for everyone. The employees have to be fairly treated and well compensated. They need to be recognized and rewarded fairly for their accomplishments. They must have opportunities to learn, succeed, improve, and grow.

But any good company can offer all that. Compensation and benefits are essential to a winning relationship, but they are hardly the only thing that matters. Many studies (and my own personal experience) have shown that once people earn above a certain level, their personal fulfillment becomes just as important as their compensation. If they have a choice between one job and another, and the compensation is roughly the same, they will usually choose the job that offers the greater opportunity for growth and development.

How does a huge enterprise like Best Buy help our employees achieve success and happiness? How do we unleash the power of our people?

Let me start with how *not* to do it. Do not hire a twenty-year-old computer geek and assign him to the household appliance department. Chances are the guy knows nothing about refrigerators except as a place to keep beer and salsa. He will not be successful surrounded by white metal, stainless steel, and stovetops.

This may sound obvious, but it took us a long time to understand the importance of putting people into jobs where they can express themselves and fuel their passion. It's what we call "casting," just like casting a movie or a television show. It's about putting the right actor into the right part—finding the role where the employee can shine and where the customer will benefit from the employee's knowledge, excitement, and love for the product, whatever it is. The person could be into photography or computer technology. He or she might feel tremendous passion for audio and be able to talk for hours about the kind of bass response you achieve when you play a certain kind of music at 130 decibels through a certain kind of speaker installed in your living room or an F150 pickup truck. People care about these things!

Brian Dunn revs up one of his Best Buy audiences.

Of course, we do not hire people just because they have a passion and like to talk about it. Candidates for jobs at Best Buy go through a rigorous hiring process that includes one-on-one interviews as well as conversations with the folks they'll be working with. We're looking for people who are willing to engage with their fellow employees and with customers. They need to understand the importance of a smile and a welcome greeting. They have to be upbeat. They must have the capacity and willingness to learn on the job. And it is very important that they be able to work as part of a team.

But the "secret sauce"—the differentiator for Best Buy, and the way to really leverage that huge reservoir of people power—is enabling our employees to live their *passion*.

THE IMPORTANCE OF VALUES TO OUR FUTURE

Much of this book is about how Best Buy *became* the best in its industry. The past is certainly interesting and relevant, but what matters most is how we will *stay* the best and how we will continue to get better and better as time goes along.

As I've said, sheer size and long-term tenure on the *Fortune* list are no guarantees of future growth. They are, in fact, no guarantee of anything.

If you want proof of that, just walk into one of any number of large retail stores today. Look around. What do you see?

Are the people who work there having fun, or are they just putting in the hours?

Are they concerned about being the best they can be, or are they just getting by, doing the bare minimum?

Are they learning something new every day, or are they doing the same old things the same old way they've always done them?

Is the power of the people being unleashed, or is it all bottled up, tamped down, crushed, or ignored?

In far too many retail outlets, the answers to these questions are not the ones you would hope for. Employees seem to have no stake in the outcome of the business. They have little regard for the company that employs them. They show no enthusiasm for the work they do each day.

When I walk into one of those places, I always have one terrible thought: *Best Buy could end up just like this.*

We could. Really, we could. And, to me, that would be a fate worse than death.

How do we avoid such a dismal prospect?

You know the answer: *values.* It is our values that will keep us honest and genuine. It is our values that will help us find the best way forward. It is our values that will enable us to grow even bigger than we are today and still be the kind of company that people love and admire.

So, even with all the competitive challenges Best Buy faces and the problems of being super-big, I don't think we're in grave danger of going the way of so many other retailers. Because of our values, our people *do* care about what they do. They believe that their roles, jobs, and activities are important. They have dreams for themselves and their departments and the company as a whole. That's why when you walk into a Best Buy store, you can feel that the values are alive. You feel confidence in the people. You trust the company.

Not long ago, I was asked, "Dick, is Best Buy still a growth company?"

My response was, *Are you kidding me?* Forty-five years ago, I had no idea what this company could achieve. I feel exactly the same way today. Of course we can grow. We can transform. We can evolve. We *have* to do so.

How else but through growth and transformation can we fulfill our promise to our employees that we will give them opportunities to be all they can be? How else can we offer our customers entry into exciting new ways of living, using technology to enhance everything they do? How else can we live up to our promise to our shareholders that we will deliver an attractive return? How else can we provide our suppliers with the best possible channel to deliver their fantastic goods to the world?

So, even after all these years, we're really just getting started. We may be the biggest and best in our industry, but we can't be satisfied with that. We have to constantly set our sights higher. In fact, I have an ambitious goal for our company. I want nothing less than for Best Buy to become *the greatest retailer the world has ever known.*

That may sound crazy, but I know it's not. Remember, I told Brad that we'd reach fifty million in revenue one day, when we were just about bankrupt. He thought I was crazy, but we surpassed that figure a thousand times over. I predicted that we could beat all of our big competitors when we were just a pipsqueak. Everybody thought

I was crazy, but now all those competitors are out of business. I said that we could radically improve the consumer experience with Concept II. Most people thought that was crazy, too, but it transformed the face of the entire consumer electronics industry.

So when I say that Best Buy can become the greatest retailer the world has ever known, I know it may sound crazy. But I believe that if we work together, innovate continuously, execute brilliantly—and, most important, *faithfully adhere to the values that enabled us to get where we are today*—we can achieve that goal.

Donna often says, "Dick asks the impossible. And he gets it."

Let's not prove her wrong on this one!

HOW THE PAPERBOY—AND HIS FAMILY—WON

I STARTED THIS BOOK WITH SOME RECOLLECTIONS ABOUT what I learned as a paperboy when I was growing up in the Twin Cities. As you may remember, I was able to make enough in tips at Christmastime to buy the car I wanted, a 1950 Pontiac that I dubbed the Green Hornet. That was a pleasing outcome for me, but it's not actually the end of the story when it comes to my paperboy experience.

Fast-forward about twenty years. I was building the company, which was still Sound of Music. We had gone public. Sandy and I were creating a satisfying life for ourselves, our family, and the company.

One Saturday morning I was alone at home, doing some work at my desk, when I heard the doorbell ring. I opened the front door and there stood a young man of ten or eleven years old, just about the age I was when I started my paper route.

"Hello," he said. And stood there.

I had never seen the boy before, so I asked him who he was and what he wanted.

"My name is Jeff," he said. "I'm collecting."

"Collecting for what?" I asked.

"The paper," he said.

"OK," I said. "How much do I owe you?"

Jeff, the paperboy, looked at me quizzically, as if he was hoping I knew the amount. "I'm not really sure…," he said. He pulled a book of stubs from his jacket and started thumbing through them, trying to add up the amount. "Ummm . . ."

The boy obviously had no idea how much I owed him or what period that would cover.

"Come in for a minute, young man," I said. "I used to be a paperboy. Let me share some ideas with you that I think will help you organize your route."

"What?" he asked. I don't know if he was pleased or terrified.

"I can show you how to be more successful at delivering papers and even more successful at satisfying your customers," I said. "Come on in."

Well, I'm not sure if that young man really wanted to improve his business, but he came in anyway. I spent about an hour with him. I showed him how to set up a route sheet, the best way to organize his customer information, and how to prepare for his collections. I gave him some important tips on dealing with customers. "Call every customer by name," I said. "Keep the paper dry. Be on time. Know how much each customer owes."

At the end of our discussion, Jeff thanked me for helping him. I paid him for what we owed and wished him good luck, and he went on his way.

Fast-forward another fifteen years. Now we were Best Buy, and the company was taking off into the stratosphere. One Saturday evening, Sandy and I attended a charity function in Minneapolis. A gentleman about my age came up, tapped me on the shoulder, and introduced himself.

"You know, Mr. Schulze," he said, "I've always wanted to meet you. You're kind of famous around our house."

"Oh, really?" I asked. "Why is that?"

"Well, you may not even remember this," he said, "but many years ago, my son, Jeff, was your paperboy. One Saturday, he came by to collect and didn't know how much you owed him. You were kind enough to invite him into your home and help him make a better plan for managing his business."

"I remember that very well," I said.

"When Jeff came home that day, he told me about your conversation. I was pretty impressed. I said to my wife, 'You know, if Mr. Schulze is kind enough and interested enough to help our son understand how to manage his paper route better, he's probably a solid businessman himself. Let's buy some shares in his company.'"

That's what he did. He purchased a hundred shares of Sound of Music stock at $3.30 per share. As we grew and became Best Buy, Jeff's Dad hung on to his investment and its value grew. In fact, the stock split five times. By the time Jeff was ready for college, that $330 investment had turned into $34,000. It paid for Jeff's college education.

I can't tell you how special that story made me feel. I thanked the father for sharing his story. I told him how much I appreciated knowing that the small amount of time I had invested in Jeff had paid off so handsomely for the whole family. And I said that I wished his son Jeff wonderful success in life.

I wish the same for you.

ACKNOWLEDGMENTS

MANY PEOPLE HELPED CREATE THIS BOOK, AND I thank them all for their efforts. They provided facts, insights, and recollections that have made the book richer, more complete, and more accurate than it might have been without their contributions.

In particular, I want to thank the two CEOs who succeeded me, Brad Anderson and Brian Dunn, for their enthusiastic participation. Thanks to Elliot Kaplan and Al Lenzmeier, who have been with me and the Best Buy enterprise for so many successful years, for their great contributions. Several directors, past and present, offered their valuable thoughts and recollections: Matthew Paull, Frank Trestman, Hatim Tyabi, and Jim Wetherbe. I was also fortunate to have the participation of many senior leaders, past and present, including Shari Ballard, Pat Matre, Sean Skelley, Robert Stephens, and Mike Vitelli. Thanks, too, to my friend Jack Tymann, for his help. Donna Mankowsi, my executive assistant, deserves a special thanks. As always, I could not have achieved this without her support.

I must especially thank the team that worked closely with me to develop, create, and produce the book—starting with Susan Marcinelli, Senior VP, Innovation and Leadership Development, who brilliantly spearheaded the effort from start to finish. Susan led the internal team—which included Bill Anderson, Matt Holz, Jen Hazelton, Natalie Albers, and many others—that helped with research, fact checking, the creation of supporting materials, and a host of other valuable tasks. Susan also worked closely with John Butman and his team at Idea Platforms, Inc.—Anna Weiss, Hannah Alpert–Abrams, and Julia Pressman—who worked for more than a year to help shape and structure the book, edit our many conversations into the final text, and produce the finished product.

Finally, I want to thank my family for their support, both throughout the years and in developing this book. My daughter, Susan Hoff, provided a great deal of valuable information, and she—along with her siblings Debra, Nancy, and Rick—encouraged me in this effort. Above all, thanks go to my wife, Maureen, for her expert editorial contributions, as well as for her constant support and encouragement.

There are many, many others who helped with the book and literally hundreds of thousands of people who, over the years, have helped to make Best Buy the amazing enterprise it is today. To all, I offer my thanks and gratitude.

APPENDICES

BEST BUY VALUES EVALUATION CRITERIA

The following tables provide detail about the specific behaviors associated with our four values—what it looks like when people are *not* living the value, when they *are* living it, and when they are helping to teach the value to others. These criteria are used as part of our performance evaluation process for all Best Buy employees.

Have fun while being the best

VALUE GOALS: SAMPLE BEHAVIORS REFERENCE SHEET			
VALUE	NOT LIVING	LIVING	TEACHING
Having fun while being the best	• Does not create an inclusive environment; takes away from interactions • Focuses on roadblocks and is generally negative • Avoids work-related team activities • Does not enjoy being at work • Likes to have fun but does not contribute significantly to team output • Blames others • Withdraws from interactions; not aligned with team's vision • Seeks results at the expense of others • Does not recognize or ensure that "fun" activities are inclusive of everyone and how they might view fun	• Seeks to understand others' definitions of fun and provides diversity in activities • Views and approaches things in a positive manner • Continually raises performance standards • Develops solutions to problems • Builds strong working relationships • Values and offers education/learning opportunities for everyone to celebrate differences and how they contribute to company success	• Motivates and pushes the team to excellence • Continually adds energy to interactions • Drives toward resolution • Ensures that all learning activities are fun and high energy • Provides consistent messages in department meetings or other settings about the value of celebrating and enjoying the differences in all employees and customers

Learn from challenge and change

VALUE GOALS: SAMPLE BEHAVIORS REFERENCE SHEET			
VALUE	NOT LIVING	LIVING	TEACHING
Learn from challenge and change	• Avoids seeking feedback • Denies feedback when offered or takes it personally • Derails positive efforts of change or resists change • Avoids challenging assumptions • Challenges assumptions in a confrontational manner • Avoids uncomfortable situations • Does not share information—leverages information as power • Does not share opinions from his or her area of expertise • Avoids addressing and driving solutions • Does not effectively mediate tension or conflict among different employees	• Gives constructive feedback • Takes feedback well and applies it going forward • Asks others for feedback • Respectfully challenges assumptions • Adapts well to change • Accepts change as a growth opportunity • Responds quickly to business needs • Seeks and shares best practices • Raises difficult issues; disagrees respectfully • Seeks opportunities that are outside the scope • Continually looks for opportunities to improve • Actively engages and welcomes a variety of diverse perspectives in resolving problems	• Understands and applies change management techniques • Respectfully challenges assumptions and engages others in dialogue about issues • Embraces change as a growth opportunity • Adapts well to change and helps others adapt • Helps others understand business case for change • Continually looks for and acts on opportunities to improve • Looks to every opportunity/interaction as a learning opportunity • Articulates how they have written themselves in to the "change" story • Understands and shares lessons of past, reality of present, and consequences for the future • Effectively interacts with a wide range of diverse individuals or groups and welcomes opportunities to be immersed in environments that are unfamiliar

Show respect, humility, and integrity

VALUE GOALS: SAMPLE BEHAVIORS REFERENCE SHEET			
VALUE	NOT LIVING	LIVING	TEACHING
Show respect, humility, and integrity	• Dismisses some points of view • Assumes negative intent • Treats people differently because of their status • Has fun at the expense of others • Assumes "my way is the only way" • Aligns only with those who "are like me" • Actions conflict with statements • Blindsides others • Avoids partnering with others • Takes credit for others' work • Takes shortcuts at the expense of others in driving for results • Does not demonstrate tangible examples of how he or she creates an environment that welcomes a variety of perspectives	• Appreciates the vast knowledge and capabilities of others • Respects and values the contributions of others • Solicits ideas from others • Listens and acknowledges others' ideas • Treats people fairly • Interacts with others in an honest and straight-forward manner • Walks the talk • Prefers to "ask" versus "tell"; seeks to understand • Assumes positive intent • Asks for help when necessary • Understands how employees differ in the way they experience the work environment and consistently seeks input	• Listens and understands others' ideas • Acts on opportunities to educate others on your work • Articulates work through the eyes of others/customers • Encourages others to share point of view • Creates an environment where others walk away from a challenging situation feeling positive, heard, empowered • Ensures that diverse perspectives are included on action-planning teams (like Viewpoint) and coaches employees on ways to invite a variety of perspectives on problem solving or improvement opportunities

Unleash the power of our people

VALUE GOALS: SAMPLE BEHAVIORS REFERENCE SHEET			
VALUE	NOT LIVING	LIVING	TEACHING
Unleash the power of our people	• Does not allow or trust people to do their jobs • Dictates how people should do their jobs • Micromanages employees/peers • Does not recognize the value of others • Does not partner well with others • Works in a silo • Fails to seek input from others • Does not have clear examples that demonstrate an understanding of each employee's strengths	• Encourages diversity of ideas and strengths • Articulates how employees contribute to the goals of the team/company • Shows commitment to individual and team engagement • Trusts others to do their jobs in their own ways • Recognizes the values of others • Helps others understand where to add value • Gives others honest, thoughtful, and constructive feedback • Shows how diverse employees participate in important projects and assignments	• Drives team engagement • Mentors peers • Positions others to do their best work • Leverages and/or engages others to accomplish goals • Utilizes the virtuous teaching cycle to share power in decision-making • Has demonstrated a TPOV on diversity to his or her team and how it contributes to helping each employee use his or her talents and strengths in support of the company mission

SOME IMPORTANT DATES
IN THE BEST BUY STORY

January 2, 1941	I'm born three minutes after my twin sister, Judie.
May 1958	I graduate from St. Paul Central High School and join the Air National Guard.
Fall 1959	I begin to work for my dad.
June 1962	I marry Sandra Jeanne Larkin.
1965	Our daughter Susan is born.
1966	I open the first three Sound of Music stores in the Twin Cities.
1968	Our daughter Debra is born.
1969	Sound of Music goes public in an "over the counter" sale.
1971	Our daughter Nancy is born.
1972	Our son Richard is born.
1973	Brad Anderson joins Sound of Music as a commissioned salesperson.
1979	Sound of Music *almost* declares bankruptcy.
June 14, 1981	A tornado destroys the Roseville Sound of Music store, and we have our first glimpse of the future business model.
1983	Sound of Music *almost* declares bankruptcy—again. We open the first Best Buy superstore, in Burnsville, Minnesota.

1985	Allen Lenzmeier joins Best Buy as CFO. We raise $8 million in our first public offering on NASDAQ. Brian Dunn joins Best Buy as a sales associate.
February 1986	Highland Superstores Inc. announces its entry into Minnesota, and we declare war. Schaak Electronics closes its twenty-one stores and liquidates assets.
May 1986	Pacific Stereo files for Chapter 11 bankruptcy.
November 1986	Best Buy opens three stores in Milwaukee.
Spring 1987	Highland enters Minneapolis and Milwaukee with three superstores each.
July 20, 1987	Best Buy begins trading on the New York Stock Exchange.
1989	We unveil Concept II and introduce the Yellow Tag logo. In October, our first Concept II store opens in Rockford, Illinois. No more commissioned sales force!
1990	Best Buy continues to expand, challenging Highland in Dallas. In May, Highland retreats from Milwaukee.
April 1991	Highland retreats from the Twin Cities. We throw a party.
August 25, 1992	Highland retreats from Chicago and files for bankruptcy.

September 1992	Best Buy successfully opens stores in Chicago.
1993	We open our first megastore. Best Buy reaches its first $1 billion in sales. Jackets for everyone!
1994	We establish the Best Buy Children's Foundation.
1995	Best Buy expands to the coasts. We now operate in twenty-seven states. We open our first Concept III stores in Baltimore and Washington, D.C. As Christmas nears, we face the computer debacle.
March 1996	We hire Andersen Consulting to help improve our systems.
1999	Best Buy ranks twenty-fifth on *Business Week*'s 50 Best Performers list. *Fortune* magazine names us one of the top ten stocks of the decade. I am named Entrepreneur of the Year. In February, I donate $50 million to the University of St. Thomas.
2000	Best Buy operates in thirty-nine states. Best Buy acquires Magnolia Hi-Fi. In June, www.bestbuy.com goes live.
2001	We acquire MusicLand and its brands Media Play, On Cue, Sam Goody, and Suncoast. We also acquire Future Shop in Canada.

June 22, 2001	Sandy passes away.
January 18, 2002	I marry Maureen Green.
Summer 2002	Best Buy headquarters move to a new facility in Richfield, Minnesota. In June, I step down as CEO and Brad Anderson becomes CEO. Best Buy acquires Geek Squad.
2003	We acquire our first global company, in Shanghai, China. We launch Best Buy Canada and announce our intention to sell MusicLand.
2004	Best Buy rolls out Geek Squad.
2005	We establish "customer-centric" stores.
2007	We establish Magnolia in key stores. In China, we open our first retail store (in Shanghai) and acquire Jiangsu Five Star Appliance. We also acquire Pacific Sales Kitchen & Bath.
2008	Best Buy acquires Speakeasy, Inc., which offers broadband, voice, data, and information technology services to small businesses. In November, Circuit City files for Chapter 11.
2009	In January, Circuit City liquidation begins. Best Buy acquires Napster, Inc.
June 24, 2009	Brian Dunn is named CEO.

INDEX